fasting

Jentezen Franklin

CHARISMA
HOUSE

Most CHARISMA HOUSE BOOK GROUP products are available at special quantity discounts for bulk purchase for sales promotions, premiums, fund-raising, and educational needs. For details, write Charisma House Book Group, 600 Rinehart Road, Lake Mary, Florida 32746, or telephone (407) 333-0600.

FASTING by Jentezen Franklin
Published by Charisma House
Charisma Media/Charisma House Book Group
600 Rinehart Road
Lake Mary, Florida 32746
www.charismahouse.com

Unless otherwise noted, all Scripture quotations are from the New King James Version of the Bible. Copyright © 1979, 1980, 1982 by Thomas Nelson, Inc., publishers. Used by permission.

Scripture quotations marked AMP are from the Amplified Bible. Old Testament copyright © 1965, 1987 by the Zondervan Corporation. The Amplified New Testament copyright © 1954, 1958, 1987 by the Lockman Foundation. Used by permission.

Scripture quotations marked KJV are from the King James Version of the Bible.

Scripture quotations marked NAS are from the New American Standard Bible, copyright © 1960, 1962, 1963, 1968, 1971, 1972, 1973, 1975, 1977, 1995 by The Lockman Foundation. Used by permission. (www.Lockman.org)

Scripture quotations marked NIV are from the Holy Bible, New International Version. Copyright © 1973, 1978, 1984, International Bible Society. Used by permission.

Some names of persons mentioned in this book have been changed to protect privacy; any similarity between individuals described in this book to individuals known to readers is purely coincidental.

Cover design by Justin Evans

Design Director: Bill Johnson

Visit the author's website at www.jentezenfranklin.org.

International Standard Book Number: 978-1-62136-619-5
E-book ISBN: 978-1-59979-358-0

The Library of Congress has cataloged the previous edition as:

Franklin, Jentezen, 1962-
    Fasting / Jentezen Franklin.
        p. cm.
    ISBN-13: 978-1-59979-258-3
    ISBN-10: 0-9759594-8-4
    1. Fasting--Religious aspects--Christianity. I. Title.
    BV5055.F73 2008
    248.4'7--dc22

                                                2007035680

While the author has made every effort to provide accurate telephone numbers and Internet addresses at the time of publication, neither the publisher nor the author assumes any responsibility for errors or for changes that occur after publication.

This publication has been translated in Spanish under the title *El ayuno*, copyright © 2008 by Jentezen Franklin, published by Casa Creación, a Charisma Media company. All rights reserved.

Previously published by Jentezen Franklin Ministries as *Fasting: The Private Discipline That Brings Public Reward*, ISBN 0-9718254-9-1, copyright © 2004, and *Fasting: Opening a Door to God's Promises*, ISBN 0-9759594-8-4, copyright © 2006.

The material contained in this book is provided for informational purposes only. It is not intended to diagnose, provide medical advice, or take the place of medical advice and treatment from your personal physician. The author in no way claims to be a medical doctor. Readers are advised to consult qualified health professionals regarding fasting and/or treatment of their specific medical problems. Neither the publisher nor the author is responsible for any possible consequences from any person reading or following the information in this book. If readers are taking prescription medications, they should consult their physicians and not take themselves off medicines without the proper supervision of a physician.

16 17 18 19 20 — 9 8 7 6 5 4 3

Printed in the United States of America

Affectionately dedicated to my deceased father, Billy D. Franklin, my foundation, who shaped my life.

This book is also dedicated to all the members of our Free Chapel and Kingdom Connection family who faithfully join us in our First Fruits Fast each year. We rejoice with you in all that God has done and will do as we seek Him together.

Acknowledgments

I wish to express my deepest appreciation to my wife, Cherise, for her constant support and encouragement, and to my dear children, Courteney, Caressa, Caroline, Connar, and Drake.

To Richie Hughes for his infusion of energy to get this book done.

To Susan Page for her tireless and wholehearted help.

To Tomi Kaiser for her ability to weave sermon stories and transcripts together to help make this book.

To my mother, Katie Franklin Lancaster, for modeling to me a fasting lifestyle.

To the Free Chapel congregation. Thanks for dreaming with me.

To the Kingdom Connection partners and friends for their support and prayers.

To all the dedicated editors on my ministry staff. Your creativity and attention to detail are a blessing. Thank you for helping me utilize the printed page in order to reach more souls for the kingdom of God.

Contents

SECTION 2
Opening a Door to God's Promises

Foreword

I count it a privilege to call Jentezen Franklin my friend publicly and privately. Many who minister have great public platforms, but not all of them have private discipline.

From years of friendship with Jentezen, I know there are certain times in the week when I can call his private line that connects to his private place where he's preparing for public ministry. I also know every January, I can call with my urgent prayer request, knowing he and his church will be on their twenty-one-day annual fast. I encourage you to read this book not just for what it will do for you publicly, but most of all privately.

—Tommy Tenney
God Chasers Network

Section 1

The Private Discipline
That Brings Public Reward

Blessed are those who hunger and thirst for righteousness, for they shall be filled.

—MATTHEW 5:6

What Is the Secret?

The question usually comes from someone with a genuine desire for deeper intimacy with the Lord and knowledge of God's perfect will. For me, fasting has been the secret to obtaining open doors, miraculous provision, favor, and the tender touch of God upon my life. I was on a three-day fast when God called me to preach. I was on a twenty-one-day fast when our ministry received its first million-dollar gift. When I was an evangelist, my brother and I traveled together. We would rotate our preaching nights. On my night off, I would fast all day for him. On his night off, he fasted all day for me. We went from obscurity to doors opening all over the world through the power of fasting. Every assignment has a birthplace. When God has placed a dream inside you that only He can make possible, you need to fast and pray. Good or bad, what's in you will come out only when you fast and pray.

Now that I'm a pastor, our church begins each year with a twenty-one-day fast. From those early years of ministry until this day, fasting has become a lifestyle. When I feel myself growing dry spiritually, when I don't sense that cutting-edge anointing, or when I need a fresh encounter with God, fasting is the secret key that unlocks heaven's door and slams shut the gates of hell.

The discipline of fasting releases the anointing, the favor, and the blessing of God in the life of a Christian. As you read this book, I will show you the power of the threefold cord. I will show you how every major biblical character fasted. I will teach you how to fast. Most importantly, as you read this book, you are going to develop a hunger to fast. I don't know about you, but there are some things that I desire more than food. "Blessed are those who hunger and thirst for righteousness, for they shall be filled" (Matt. 5:6).

Since you are reading this book, you are probably not content to go through this year the way you went through last year. You know there's more. You know there is an assignment for your life. You know there are things that God desires to release in your life, and there is a genuine desperation for those things gripping your heart. It was for you, and for those like you, that this book was written. Now I want to invite you to join this marvelous journey.

> Beware of practicing your righteousness before men to be noticed by them; otherwise you have no reward with your Father who is in heaven.
>
> So when you give to the poor, do not sound a trumpet before you, as the hypocrites do in the synagogues and in the streets, so that they may be honored by men. Truly I say to you, they have their reward in full. But when you give to the poor, do not let your left hand know what your right hand is doing, so that your giving will be in secret; and your Father who sees what is done in secret will reward you.
>
> When you pray, you are not to be like the hypocrites; for they love to stand and pray in the synagogues and on the street corners so that they may be seen by men. Truly I say to you, they have their reward in full. But you,

when you pray, go into your inner room, close your door and pray to your Father who is in secret, and your Father who sees what is done in secret will reward you. And when you are praying, do not use meaningless repetition as the Gentiles do, for they suppose that they will be heard for their many words.

So do not be like them; for your Father knows what you need before you ask Him. Pray, then, in this way:

"Our Father who is in heaven,

Hallowed be Your name.

Your kingdom come.

Your will be done,

On earth as it is in heaven.

Give us this day our daily bread.

And forgive us our debts, as we also have forgiven our debtors.

And do not lead us into temptation, but deliver us from evil. [For Yours is the kingdom and the power and the glory forever. Amen.]"

For if you forgive others for their transgressions, your heavenly Father will also forgive you. But if you do not forgive others, then your Father will not forgive your transgressions.

Whenever you fast, do not put on a gloomy face as the hypocrites do, for they neglect their appearance so that they will be noticed by men when they are fasting. Truly I say to you, they have their reward in full. But you, when you fast, anoint your head and wash your face so that your fasting will not be noticed by men, but by your Father who is in secret; and your Father who sees what is done in secret will reward you.

—MATTHEW 6:1–18, NASU

As the deer pants for the water brooks, so pants my soul for You, O God. My soul thirsts for God, for the living God. When shall I come and appear before God? My tears have been my food day and night, while they continually say to me, "Where is your God?"

—Psalm 42:1–3

Chapter 1

Fasting for Your Breakthrough

What is fasting? Since there are so many misconceptions about it, I first want to clarify what fasting—biblical fasting—is not. Fasting is not merely going without food for a period of time. That is dieting—maybe even starving—but fasting it is not. Nor is fasting something done only by fanatics. I really want to drive that point home. Fasting is not to be done only by religious monks alone in a cave somewhere. The practice of fasting is not limited to ministers or to special occasions.

Stated simply, biblical fasting is refraining from food for a spiritual purpose. Fasting has always been a normal part of a relationship with God. As expressed by the impassioned plea of David in Psalm 42, fasting brings one into a deeper, more intimate and powerful relationship with the Lord.

When you eliminate food from your diet for a number of days, your spirit becomes uncluttered by the things of this world and amazingly sensitive to the things of God. As David stated, "Deep calls unto deep" (Ps. 42:7). David was fasting. His hunger and thirst for God were greater than his natural desire for food. As a result, he reached a place where he could cry out from the depths of his spirit to the depths of God, even in the midst of his trial. Once you've experienced even a glimpse of that kind of intimacy with our God—our Father, the holy Creator of the universe—and the countless rewards and blessings that follow, your whole perspective will change. You will soon realize that fasting is a secret source of power that is overlooked by many.

A threefold cord is not quickly broken.
—ECCLESIASTES 4:12

During the years that Jesus walked this earth, He devoted time to teaching His disciples the principles of the kingdom of God, principles that conflict with those of this world. In the Beatitudes, specifically in Matthew 6, Jesus provided the pattern by which each of us is to live as a child of God. That pattern addressed three specific duties of a Christian: giving, praying, and fasting. Jesus said, "*When* you give…" and "*When* you pray…" and "*When* you fast." He made it clear that fasting, like giving and praying, was a normal part of Christian life. As much attention should be given to fasting as is given to giving and to praying.

> The three duties of every Christian
> are giving, praying, and fasting.

Solomon, when writing the books of wisdom for Israel, made the point that a cord, or rope, braided with three strands is not easily broken (Eccles. 4:12). Likewise, when giving, praying, and fasting are practiced together in the life of a believer, it creates a type of threefold cord that is not easily broken. In fact, as I'll show you in a moment, Jesus took it even further by saying, "Nothing will be impossible" (Matt. 17:20).

Could we be missing our greatest breakthroughs because we fail to fast? Remember the thirtyfold, sixtyfold, and hundredfold return Jesus spoke of (Mark 4:8, 20)? Look at it this way: when you pray, you can release that thirtyfold return, but when both prayer and giving are part of your life, I believe that releases the sixtyfold blessing. But when all three—giving, praying, and fasting—are part of your life, that hundredfold return can be released!

If that's the case, you have to wonder what blessings are not being released. What answers to prayer are not getting through? What bondages are not being broken because we fail to fast?

Matthew tells the story of a father who had a demon-possessed son. For years he watched helplessly as his son suffered with severe convulsions. As he grew older, the attacks became so severe that the boy would often throw himself into an open fire or a trench of water. A suicidal spirit tormented him constantly; the situation became life-threatening.

Having exhausted every attempt to cure the boy—even taking him to the disciples with no avail—the father's plight seemed impossible. Then he heard that Jesus was near. Going to the Master, he cried, "Lord, have mercy on my son: for he is lunatick, and sore vexed: for ofttimes he falleth into the fire, and oft into the water. And I brought him to thy disciples, and they could not cure him" (Matt. 17:15, KJV).

When the boy was brought to Jesus, the Bible says He "rebuked the devil; and he departed out of him: and the child was cured from that very hour" (v. 18, KJV). But what made the difference? After all, Matthew 10:1 records that Jesus had already given the disciples power to cast out evil spirits and to heal every disease. So why couldn't the disciples cast out the demon and cure the boy?

That's what they wanted to know, too, so later that night, when they were alone with Jesus, they asked Him. Jesus replied, "Because of your unbelief: for verily I say unto you, If ye have faith as a grain of mustard seed, ye shall say unto this mountain, Remove hence to yonder place; and it shall remove; and nothing shall be impossible unto you. Howbeit this kind goeth not out but by prayer and fasting" (Matt. 17:20–21, KJV).

Now, I've read that passage many times, and I've even taught from it on occasion. But each time, I've focused on the statement "and nothing shall be impossible unto you." I think a lot of people stop right there, but Jesus didn't because He knew there was more—much more.

> When you faithfully follow the three duties
> of a Christian, God rewards you openly.

See, that funny little word *howbeit* is the connection—it's the key that unlocks the power in the statement "nothing shall be impossible unto you." Jesus told the disciples they needed faith, even faith as small as a tiny seed. But that wasn't all. Long before this incident, the Holy Spirit led Jesus into the wilderness, where He spent forty days and forty nights, taking no food. "Howbeit this kind goeth not out but by prayer and fasting." For Jesus, casting out that stubborn demon wasn't impossible.

If Jesus could have accomplished all He came to do without fasting, why would He fast? The Son of God fasted because He knew there were supernatural things that could only be released that way. How much more should fasting be a common practice in our lives?

Fasting Is for Everyone

Perhaps you're thinking, "I still don't know how fasting can really be for me." According to the words of Jesus, it is the duty of every disciple and every believer to fast. When addressing the Pharisees as to why His disciples did not fast, Jesus replied, "Can you make the friends of the bridegroom fast while the bridegroom is with them? But the days will come when the bridegroom will be taken away from them; then they will fast in those days" (Luke 5:34–35).

Then they will fast. Jesus didn't expect His disciples to do something He hadn't done as well. Jesus fasted, and according to the words of Peter, Jesus is our example in all things (1 Pet. 2:21).

> A disciple is not above his teacher, but everyone who is perfectly trained will be like his teacher.
>
> —LUKE 6:40

There's another vital point that I want you to see in Matthew 6: God delights in giving rewards. Not only that, but He says that when giving, praying, and fasting are practiced in your life, He will "reward you openly."

A good example of such open reward can be found in Daniel. While in Babylonian captivity, his fasting—even partial fasting of certain foods—brought about the open reward of God, who blessed Daniel with wisdom beyond that of anyone else in that empire.

Later, in chapter 10, Daniel was grieved and burdened with the revelation he had received for Israel. He ate no choice breads or meats and drank no wine for three weeks. Then he describes the angel that was sent to him—which had been *delayed* by the prince of Persia for twenty-one days—with the answers Daniel sought. His fast broke the power of the delayer and released the angels of God so that God's purposes could be revealed and served.

This is just the tip of the iceberg. As you read on, I will show you how this threefold cord works in every area of your life. Do you desire to know God's will for your life, whom you should marry, or what you should do in a critical situation? I'll show you how fasting brings you to a place of being able to clearly hear God's will.

Fasting also causes God to target your children. You would be amazed at the testimonies we have heard about fasting. It also brings health and healing to your body, as well as financial prosperity and the blessings of God.

Whether you desire to be closer to God or are in need of great breakthroughs in your life, remember that nothing shall be impossible to you. Fasting is truly a secret source of power!

Then Jesus, being filled with the Holy Spirit, returned from the Jordan and was led by the Spirit into the wilderness, being tempted for forty days by the devil. And in those days He ate nothing, and afterward, when they had ended, He was hungry.

—LUKE 4:1–2

Chapter 2

Dethroning King Stomach

If you are like others who have heard me speak on even a portion of what was covered in the first chapter, by now you are beginning to realize how crucial the practice of fasting is in the life of every believer. But as a part of that threefold cord of normal Christian duties, why is it so often overlooked? I believe the primary reason is one that has plagued mankind since the dawn of creation.

You see, fasting means crucifying what I refer to as "King Stomach." And in case you don't know who King Stomach is, just move this book out of the way, look down, and introduce yourself. You've probably already heard him rumble in disagreement a time or two since you began reading this book!

Every year our entire congregation at Free Chapel participates in a twenty-one-day fast. Without fail, folks share with me that they feel like eating everything in sight that last week or so before beginning the fast. But that's OK. Once you make that decision to fast, even if it's just for a day, God sees the desire of your heart. He will provide you with the grace to endure and see the breakthroughs you need come to pass. However, you will have to choose to dethrone that "dictator within."

> You will have to choose to dethrone that "dictator within."

It has been said that the way to a man's heart is through his stomach. Most women have come to know it, but we need to realize that the devil knows it, too! Some people—specifically Christians—could be the geographical location of the "bottomless pit"! Consider for just a moment what has happened to the human race while under the rule of King Stomach.

We can start at the beginning, all the way back in the Garden of Eden. The Bible records:

> The LORD God planted a garden eastward in Eden; and there he put the man whom he had formed. And out of the ground made the LORD God to grow every tree that is pleasant to the sight, and good for food; the tree of life also in the midst of the garden, and the tree of the knowledge of good and evil.... And the LORD God commanded the man, saying, Of every tree of the garden thou mayest freely eat: but of the tree of the knowledge of good and evil, thou shalt not eat of it: for in the day that thou eatest thereof thou shalt surely die.
>
> —GENESIS 2:8–9, 16–17, KJV

Seems straightforward enough, right? But the serpent was cunning and convinced Eve that she should eat from the forbidden tree, assuring her that she would not die. "So when the woman saw that the tree was good for food...she took of its fruit and ate. She also gave to her husband with her, and he ate" (Gen. 3:6).

And with that one meal, Adam and Eve immediately went from peacefully enjoying God's presence in the cool of the garden to fearfully hiding from His presence among the trees of the garden.

They literally ate themselves out of house and home. They ate themselves out of the will of God for their lives. They ate themselves out of God's provision and plan for their lives and out of His magnificent presence. But their stomachs were temporarily satisfied, and we still suffer the consequences of their appetites today.

King Stomach's Reign

When speaking of the sins of Sodom and Gomorrah, people usually focus on the rampant homosexuality in those cities. But that is not all the Bible teaches. The Lord said to Israel through the prophet Ezekiel: "Look, this was the iniquity of your sister Sodom: She and her daughter had pride, fullness of food, and abundance of idleness; neither did she strengthen the hand of the poor and needy. And they were haughty and committed abomination before Me; therefore I took them away as I saw fit" (Ezek. 16:49–50).

They ate themselves out of the will of God for their lives.

The first thing you may notice is that there was no giving (poor and needy) and no praying (pride and idleness). But it is interesting to note that the inhabitants of those cities were not only guilty of homosexuality, according to the account in Genesis, but as we see here, they were also guilty of gluttony (fullness of food). Along with their other sins, their excessive loyalty to King Stomach carried them right into damnation!

Another brilliant example of one in whom King Stomach was high and lifted up is Esau, the son of Isaac and Rebekah. As was the custom, Esau was endowed with the special birthright of the firstborn male child. That birthright brought with it his father's special blessing and certain privileges. It automatically insured that Esau would receive a double portion of all his father's estate. It was a blessing from God and not to be taken lightly.

Esau was a hunter. His father delighted in him because of the abundance of meat he brought to the table. But when Esau returned from the field one day, perhaps having had no success in the hunt, he was hungry. His brother, Jacob, was about to have a simple meal of red lentils and bread, so Esau, insisting he was famished, begged Jacob for the same meal. When he impulsively agreed to exchange his birthright for it, "Jacob gave Esau bread and stew of lentils; then he ate and drank, arose, and went his way. Thus Esau despised his birthright" (Gen. 25:34).

Esau sold his coveted birthright because of his allegiance to King Stomach. God had a plan, a destiny, a will for Esau's life, but his lust for food and instant gratification was more important. The writer of Hebrews used strong terms to warn against becoming like Esau: "Lest anyone fall short of the grace of God...lest there be any fornicator or profane person like Esau, who for one morsel of food sold his birthright. For you know that afterward, when he wanted to inherit the blessing, he was rejected, for he found no place for repentance, though he sought it diligently with tears" (Heb. 12:15–17).

When God delivered the Israelites after four hundred years of oppressive slavery in Egypt, millions of Israelites and a "mixed multitude" of others were miraculously led through the Red Sea on their way to the Promised Land. God provided for their every need on the journey, even feeding them bread from heaven daily. This manna provided such a perfectly balanced diet that there was not one sick or feeble person among them for forty years—with no doctors, drugstores, or hospitals. It filled their bellies and kept their bodies healthy and strong. However, "the mixed multitude who were among them yielded to intense craving; so the children of Israel also wept again and said: 'Who will give us meat to eat? We remember the fish which we ate freely in Egypt, the cucumbers, the melons, the leeks, the onions, and the garlic; but now our whole being is dried up; there is nothing at all except this manna before our eyes'" (Num. 11:4–7).

God heard their murmuring and complaining. As any mom can attest, it is just not a good idea to get the cook mad at you. God said, "The LORD will give you meat, and you shall eat. You shall eat, not one day, nor two days, nor five days, nor ten days, nor twenty days, but for a whole month, until it comes out of your nostrils and becomes loathsome to you, because you have despised the LORD" (vv. 18–20). And He sent them quail in such a great abundance they stacked it two and a half feet deep! And they ate and ate, and while the meat was in their mouths, thousands of them died and were buried there. And according to verse 34, that place became known as Kibroth Hattaavah, which means "The Graves of Lusters," as a memorial to those who ate themselves right out of the Promised Land.

The commentator Matthew Henry wrote, "Those who are under the power of a carnal mind, will have their lusts fulfilled, though it be to the certain damage and ruin of their precious souls."[1] I want you to understand that there are some "promised lands" and some "promises" that God has for you. In fact, we have an entire book of promises, but some of them will never be realized as long as King Stomach rules your appetite and controls your life. God had supernatural blessings to pour out on the Israelites in the wilderness, but they preferred their carnal appetites. Likewise, God wants to pour out supernatural blessings in our lives, but they will never be realized if we are not willing to seek Him in fasting and prayer.

> God knows there is never a
> convenient time to fast.

In our busy lives there is always a holiday, birthday, office lunch, or something that creates a bump in the road, so we talk ourselves out of beginning a fast. My advice to you, based on personal experience, is to just jump in and do it, and everything else will take care of itself! If you have never fasted before, just do it for one day and you will see what I mean.

The reason we fast corporately at Free Chapel at the beginning of every year is based on principles that have been adapted from Dr. Bob Rodgers's book *101 Reasons to Fast*. There are three reasons starting the year with a fast is a good practice. First, by doing so, you set the course for the rest of the year. Just as beginning your day with prayer sets the course for the rest of the day and covers anything that may happen, the same is true of beginning the year with a fast. You set the course for the entire year by what you do with those first few days of each New Year. You can carry that even further to give God the first part of every day, the first day of every week, the first portion of every dollar, and the first consideration in every decision.

Secondly, "Blessings will happen for you and your family throughout the year because you fasted in January." Even in April, June, or August, even into November when you have Thanksgiving goodies on your mind, blessings will still be finding their way to you because of your sacrifice to the Lord at the beginning of the year. In fact, it was around Thanksgiving when I got the call to go to the bank. When I arrived, a man and his wife met me and said, "Here is a million dollars for the building program." I had forgotten about the fast we had done ten months prior, but God hadn't. He not only sent someone to us with a million-dollar gift, but also someone with a $500,000 gift, a $250,000 gift, a $50,000 gift, and cumulative millions that came in regular gifts all in that same year.

This third point is so powerful. When you fast at the beginning of the year and pray, you release the principle found in Matthew 6:33: "Seek *first* the kingdom of God and His righteousness, and all these things shall be added to you" (emphasis added). If you seek Him first in the year, get ready for all these "things" to be added to your life throughout the rest of the year!

I have not departed from the commandment of His lips; I have treasured the words of His mouth more than my necessary food.

—Job 23:12

Chapter 3

How Much?
How Long?
How Healthy?

In the last chapter, I described the downfall of some who failed to dethrone King Stomach. But God's Word is full of marvelous testimonies of those who succeeded. It was during a forty-day fast that Moses received the Ten Commandments (Exod. 34:27–28). When Haman ordered the annihilation and plunder of all Jews, Esther called for all the Jews of her city to join her on a three-day fast from all food and water. As a result, the Jews were spared, Haman's vile plan was exposed, and he was hanged on the very gallows he built! (See Esther 4–7.) Hannah, greatly distressed over not being able to bear a child, "wept and did not eat," as recorded in 1 Samuel 1:7. God heard her plea, and the prophet Samuel was soon born. Judah, Ezra, the people of Nineveh, Nehemiah, David, and Anna are also among those whose fasts are noted in the Word.

Types of Fasts

The Bible records many different circumstances, types, and lengths of fasts. In addition to those I just mentioned, Joshua fasted forty days, and Daniel partially fasted twenty-one days. It is recorded that the apostle Paul was on at least two fasts: one for three days and one for fourteen days. Peter fasted three days, and, of course, we know that Jesus fasted forty days in the wilderness.

The three types of fasts found in Scripture are the absolute fast, the normal fast, and the partial fast. First, an absolute fast is extreme and should be done only for very short periods of time. On an absolute fast, you take in nothing—no food, no water. Depending on your health, this fast should be attempted only with medical consultation and supervision.

On a normal fast, you typically go without food of any kind for a certain number of days. You do drink water, and plenty of it! Depending on the length of the normal fast, you may also choose to take clear broth and juices in order to maintain your strength.

And then there is the partial fast. A partial fast can be interpreted many ways. The way it cannot be interpreted is to include that time between about 11:00 p.m. and 6:00 a.m.—when you're sleeping! A partial fast usually involves giving up particular foods and drink for an extended period of time.

The most commonly used example of a partial fast is found in the Book of Daniel. In the beginning of his captivity in Babylon, Daniel and his three companions refused to eat the choice meats and sweets from the king's table, asking instead to have only vegetables and water. They did this for ten days to prove that they would be just as healthy as the king's men. Later, in chapter 10, grieved over the plight of Israel, Daniel began another partial fast, taking no sweets, no meat, and no wine for three weeks, during which time he was focused in prayer. At the end, his prayer was answered by an angel.

The duration of fasts can vary. There are significant numbers we find in the Bible, which include three days, seven days, twenty-one days, and forty days. But there are also references to half-day fasts and twenty-four-hour fasts.

There is no real formula that I can give you to help you determine which type or length of fast is right for you. The length of time that you choose to fast should depend on your circumstances, but don't get bogged down in the details. Begin with one day from sunrise to sunset. You will be amazed at the difference even a one-day partial or normal fast will make in your life. As a teenager, I would fast all day on Sunday until after church. It made me so much more sensitive to the Lord. I would be so spiritually tuned in that it didn't matter if anyone else got a blessing that day or not—I sure did!

Don't bite off more than you can handle. There is no need to be heroic and attempt a forty-day fast if you have never fasted a day in your life. Just start. Once you discover the benefits, you'll be on your way to making it a life practice.

There are times when the Lord may impress you to go on a longer fast, but for most folks, a three-day fast is very practical. A "Daniel fast," eliminating meat, bread, and sweets for twenty-one days, is a fast just about anyone can handle as well. Some may think eliminating only those three foods from your diet for three weeks is no big deal. But if it means something to you, it will mean something to God. After all, when was the last time angels were released to speak mysteries to you like the archangel Michael spoke to Daniel?

> If it doesn't mean anything to you,
> it won't mean anything to God.

On longer fasts, I drink water, juice, and even broth when I feel I need a little extra strength. The local Chick-fil-A has grown so accustomed to our annual fasts at Free Chapel that they now readily strain their chicken noodle soup so we can buy just a cup of broth!

Practical Tips

I want to give you a few tips on fasting that I believe you will find helpful. Whenever you begin a fast, remember, if it doesn't mean anything to you, it won't mean anything to God. Without being combined with prayer and the Word, fasting is little more than dieting. But I want you to realize something very important: fasting itself is a continual prayer before God. There may be days when heaven opens and your heart is prompted to deep times of prayer. But there may be other days when your energy is sapped and you just cannot seem to focus in prayer at all. Don't condemn yourself. God sees your sacrifice. When you are fasting is not the time to sit in front of the TV. Why would you want to torture yourself with all those food advertisements anyway?

I can tell you from my own experience—it's just not a good idea! It is my normal routine to watch the news before going to bed. During the second week of my very first twenty-one-day fast, Pizza Hut introduced their new pan pizza. Without fail, during the news every night at about 11:17 p.m., those steamy images of bubbling cheese, thick crust, rich tomato sauce, and various toppings would take center stage. They would lift a slice of pizza out of that deep pan and the cheese would just ooze down. I knew where I was going at the end of that fast! I would actually look forward to those commercials! One night I was dreaming that I was about to eat one of those slices of pan pizza. That dream was so real, I remember my conscience screaming, "This isn't right! Don't do it...you've only got another week to go!" But I stuffed it in my mouth and chewed and chewed. It was so good! I woke up a few minutes later, quite startled to find nearly half my pillowcase stuffed in my mouth!

Fasting is like spring cleaning for your body!

When you begin longer fasts, it is not a good idea to gorge yourself the days before. You should actually begin tapering off your food intake in preparation. Regardless of the length of your fast, when you begin, you should try to drink at least one gallon of purified water throughout the first day. I don't recommend tap water because of the impurities it can contain. Purified or distilled water flushes the toxins and the poison out of your system, which will help you get off to a good start. It also makes you feel full! Water is the faster's best friend, so continue to drink plenty throughout the fast.

When I go on a fast, I often get a headache the first day or two. I've had a lot of people tell me that the devil gave them a headache. But more likely, it is simply your body getting rid of the toxins that have built up over a period of time. See, fasting is like spring cleaning for your body! It gives your whole digestive system a break, and, medically speaking, that is very healthy. If you experience a headache while fasting, it is a sign that you needed to fast. The headaches are the result of the impurities and poisons the body is burning for energy. After three days, the headaches usually disappear.

Whenever you fast for at least three days, your digestive system shuts down. I'll be honest with you; it is not always pleasant. Some feel sluggish, have head-aches, and can't sleep, and, let's face it, you are going to get hungry! But I want to assure you that once you get through those first couple of days, if you will keep drinking plenty of water and juice, those toxins that poison your body will get flushed out, and you will find what can only be described as a sweet place in the fast!

When I've been on an extended fast, during the first few days as my body emptied itself of toxins, I saw no angels and heard no violins. In fact, I didn't feel much like focusing on prayer and the Word. But without fail, things soon clear up, and you find a deeper place in God where the rest just does not matter.

Solomon said, "That which has been is what will be, that which is done is what will be done, and there is nothing new under the sun" (Eccles. 1:9). Though men and women of God have fasted since ancient times, today we have many new books on the shelves touting the healthy physical benefits of the practice. Even the Greek physician Hippocrates (approximately 460–377 B.C.), known as the "father of modern medicine" and whose concepts have influenced the development of medical practices for centuries, believed fasting was very healthy for the body.

In his book *101 Reasons to Fast*, Pastor Bob Rodgers cites many statements from Hippocrates and others who discovered the many medical benefits fasting can have on the body. Fasting cleans your body. As you begin a fast, you will notice a sort of coating on your tongue for a few days. It is a sign the fast is helping your body eliminate toxins. Tests have proven that the average American consumes and assimilates four pounds of chemical preservatives, coloring, stabilizers, flavorings, and other additives each year. These build up in our bodies and cause illness and disease. Periodic fasts are necessary to flush out the poisons. Fasting gives your body time to heal itself. It relieves nervousness and tension and gives your digestive system a rest. Fasting lowers your blood pressure and can lower your cholesterol.[1]

Don Colbert, MD, has researched and studied the body's need to rid itself of toxins that cause illness, disease, fatigue, and many other ailments. Because I do not attempt to cover every medical aspect and benefit of fasting in this book, I would recommend his book *Toxic Relief* for specific medical guidelines for fasting. His chapter titled "Finding Healing Through Fasting" is an excellent source of information and cautions. He says, "Fasting does not only prevent sickness. If done correctly, fasting holds amazing healing benefits to those of us who suffer illness and disease. From colds and flu to heart disease, fasting is a mighty key to healing the body."[2]

Dr. Oda H. F. Birchinger, who supervised more than seventy thousand fasts, stated, "Fasting is a royal road to healing, for anyone who agrees to take it, for recovery and regeneration of the body, mind, and spirit." He went on to say, "Fasting can heal and help rheumatism in the joints and muscles, diseases of the heart, circulation, blood vessels, stress-related exhaustion, skin diseases—including pimples and complexion problems, irregular menstrual cycles and hot flashes, disease of respiratory organs, allergies such as hay fever and other eye diseases."[3]

To test the results of fasting on the human body, Dr. Tanner, another medical doctor, decided at the age of fifty to fast forty-three days without food. He did so under strict medical supervision. At the conclusion of the fast, he was much healthier. At age sixty he fasted fifty days, and in the middle of his fast, he said he saw the unspeakable glories of God. At age seventy-seven, Dr. Tanner fasted fifty-three days, and among other things that happened, his once thin, gray hair was replaced by new black hair! It was the same color that it was when he was a young man. What's more, Dr. Tanner lived to be ninety-three years old.[4]

Fasting slows your aging process. Moses fasted often, including two forty-day fasts, and the Bible says in Deuteronomy 34:7, "Moses was one hundred and twenty years old when he died. His eyes were not dim nor his natural vigor diminished." Dr. Tanner passed on some advice from his own experiences, stating,

"When you fast, drink plenty of water."[5] Water is the great flushing agent in fasting. One of the signs that these toxins and poisons are being eliminated can be seen by the concentration of toxins in our urine. These toxins may be ten times higher than normal when you're fasting. The urine turns darker because the disease-causing poison and toxins locked in your body because of terrible diets begin to be washed out.

It is also proven that fasting sharpens your mental process and aids and improves your sight, hearing, taste, touch, smell, and all sensory faculties. Fasting breaks the addiction to junk food. Fasting can break the power of an uncontrollable appetite. Some are bound by nicotine, alcohol, and drugs, but fasting can help break those addictions.[6]

Each year I encourage all the members of Free Chapel to join us in our twenty-one-day fast. If in twenty-one days you can be a new person, why go the rest of your life feeling sick, weak, overweight, and run down? Why not take a radical step of faith? We have only one life to give to God—let's get control of our bodies and go for God with the best we have!

My sheep hear My voice, and I know them, and they follow Me. And I give them eternal life, and they shall never perish; neither shall anyone snatch them out of My hand.

—John 10:27–28

Chapter 4

Every Assignment
Has a Birthplace

I love the statement Jesus made in John 10:27: "My sheep *hear* My voice" (emphasis added). That is how He created us. He speaks to us, and we are able to hear Him speaking. Do you want to hear the voice of the Creator? Do you want to know Jesus more deeply? Do you want to know the direction He desires you to take in life? I do.

As I was completing this book, I was beginning my seventh full twenty-one-day fast since entering the ministry. I began my first one when I was just seventeen years old. My parents were always godly examples when I was growing up, so even at that young age, I was becoming aware that fasting was a part of being a true follower of Christ. If you are a parent reading this book, I want you to know that even children can begin to understand these concepts, and it is important that they learn them at a young age.

Prior to that first twenty-one-day fast at the age of seventeen, I had completed shorter ones. In fact, it was during a three-day fast that God revealed His assignment for my life. I was praying and seeking His will. That is when He called me to preach.

Every assignment, every call of God, every direction from Him starts somewhere. God has specific assignments for your life. But how do you discover them? How will you hear His voice? How will you know His will for your life, His plans for you? Whom should you marry? Where should you live? What job should you take? What mission field is calling your name?

The answer can be found in the appeal Paul made to the Romans: "Present your bodies a living sacrifice, holy, acceptable to God, which is your reasonable service" (Rom. 12:1). Remember the three Christian duties I covered in the first chapter? Giving, praying, and *fasting*. That is how you "present" your body to God as a "living" sacrifice. Fasting keeps you sensitive to His Spirit, enabling you to live holy. Paul went on to say, "And do not be conformed to this world, but be transformed by the renewing of your mind, *that you may prove what is that good and acceptable and perfect will of God*" (v. 2, emphasis added).

> Fasting keeps you sensitive to His
> Spirit, enabling You to live holy.

I am convinced that we will never walk in the perfect will of God until we seek Him through fasting. When you present your body in this manner, you open yourself up to hear from God. You will prove or discover His good and perfect will for your life. Paul was fasting when God called him and shared the assignment for his life (Acts 9:7–9). Peter was fasting on the rooftop when God gave him a new revelation and called him to take the gospel to the Gentiles (Acts 10). Fasting prepares the way for God to give you fresh revelation, fresh vision, and clear purpose.

In the Book of Joel, the Lord said, "And it shall come to pass afterward that I will pour out My Spirit on all flesh; your sons and your daughters shall prophesy, your old men shall dream dreams, your young men shall see visions" (Joel 2:28). God was going to pour out revival—*afterward*. He was revealing His will for His people—*afterward*. After what? After a fast. Israel was in sin, and God was calling His people to fast in repentance as a people: "Blow the trumpet in Zion, consecrate a *fast*, call a sacred assembly" (v. 15, emphasis added). His promise to them was to pour out revival and blessings on the land. I don't know about you, but I'm ready for those "afterward" seasons when God pours out revival, when our sons and daughters prophesy! What are we waiting for when we read scriptures like 2 Chronicles 7:14? Can you imagine if believers in America really took hold of this, if they humbled themselves (fasted) and prayed? God would heal our nation and send revival!

> Fasting is what prepares you
> for a new anointing.

But if He is going to pour out new wine, our wineskins will have to change. Jesus said, "No one puts new wine into old wineskins; or else the new wine bursts the wineskins, the wine is spilled, and the wineskins are ruined. But new wine must be put into new wineskins" (Mark 2:22). I had never seen the connection between fasting and the new wine before. But if you look at this passage, Jesus had just finished telling the Pharisees that His disciples would fast once He was gone. Fasting is what prepares you for a new anointing (v. 20). God can't put that kind of wine in old skins. If you want new wine, new miracles, new closeness, new intimacy with Him, then it's time to call a fast and shed that old skin for the new.

Fasting is a tremendous weapon and a source of power in the life of a believer. The blessings in my life are directly attributed to the fasting in my life. I am not the greatest preacher; I don't have the brilliant mind that some have, but God said He is no respecter of persons. When you honor and worship God by presenting your body as a living sacrifice through fasting, you too will know His assignments for your life.

Perhaps you are at a place of such desperation that you just cannot afford to miss God's will for your life. I have known people who were literally facing life-or-death situations. They were trapped, they were under pressure by circumstances, and they were under attack by the enemy. The only possible way to survive was to draw near to God—from whose hand no one can snatch you—to hear His voice, and to follow His plan.

Jehoshaphat, king of Judah, was in a similarly critical situation. He was a God-fearing king who found himself surrounded by a powerful enemy army. Annihilation was certain without the Lord's intervention. Scripture records that, "Jehoshaphat feared, and set himself to seek the LORD, and proclaimed a fast throughout all Judah. So Judah gathered together to ask help from the LORD; and from all the cities of Judah they came to seek the LORD.... Now all Judah, with their little ones, their wives, and their children, stood before the LORD" (2 Chron. 20:3-4, 13).

All of Judah fasted, even the women and children. They desperately needed to know the Lord's plan to defeat this great enemy army. In the midst of that assembly of fasting people, God spoke to His people through a prophet, who encouraged them, saying, "'Do not be afraid nor dismayed because of this great multitude, for the battle is not yours, but God's.... You will not need to fight in this battle. Position yourselves, stand still and see the salvation of the LORD, who is with you, O Judah and Jerusalem!' Do not fear or be dismayed; tomorrow go out against them, for the Lord is with you" (vv. 15, 17).

In the midst of the whole assembly, God told Judah exactly how that enemy army would approach and exactly what they were to do in response. They gave tremendous praise to the Lord, and He set ambushes against the enemy army and defeated them. None escaped. When the people of Judah arrived, it took them three whole days to carry away the spoil!

Do you want God to tell you what you need to do at this time in your life? Fast, worship, and seek Him. Be still and see the salvation of the Lord! They didn't even have to fight. God fought for them. The battle took one day, and God not only delivered them, but He also prospered them. It took them three days to carry off all the riches! I'm ready for some of those victories where it takes me longer to bring the victory home than it took to fight the battle! Press in like Jehoshaphat in times of great distress—you and your whole family, perhaps even your entire church. God will deliver you and show you His plan!

Satan Hates When You Fast

Satan gets disturbed—and defeated—when you decide to do more than be a Sunday-morning Christian. He has probably tried repeatedly to distract you from reading this chapter already. The devil knows fasting releases God's power.

Have you ever wondered why, of all things, Satan tempted Jesus at the end of His fast by provoking Him to turn stones into bread? Jesus had the power to do so, but He came to use His power to serve others, not Himself. Further, He was determined to complete the fast God had called Him to finish. Jesus knew that some of the benefits of fasting cannot be released otherwise—and so did the devil! When Jesus returned from that forty-day fast, He immediately began to do mighty miracles, "healing all who were oppressed by the devil" (Acts 10:38). Satan needed to get Jesus focused on His appetite because if he didn't, Jesus was going to receive power from God that would change the world!

Preparation + equipping

Remember, the enemy's agenda is to steal, kill, and destroy you (John 10:10). Do you think the enemy *wants* you to believe that nothing is impossible for you?

He knows he is defeated, but he doesn't want you to know it or to walk in that realm of God's power. That is why it is so crucial for him to get you distracted. Don't allow the enemies in your life to cause you to focus more on your appetite or circumstances than on the promises of God that are released when you employ the powerful weapon of fasting.

For you were once darkness, but now you are light in the Lord. Walk as children of light (for the fruit of the Spirit is in all goodness, righteousness, and truth), finding out what is acceptable to the Lord.

—EPHESIANS 5:8–10

Chapter 5

Swatting Flies

We begin each New Year at Free Chapel with a twenty-one-day corporate fast. Everyone participates in some measure. Some may fast one day, others three days, some a week, some even the full twenty-one days. As a body, when we all fast together over that twenty-one-day period, God is honored, and He rewards that sacrifice corporately and individually. But some people are never satisfied. I've had people testify that only *three days* into a fast for a loved one suffering with cancer, the cancer was completely cured! Another lady's son was dying from a 107-degree fever associated with his leukemia. The very first day of the fast, the boy's fever broke, and he didn't suffer a trace of brain damage!

They both received miraculous rewards from God for their sacrifices. But that just was not enough. Both of them continued fasting for the twenty-one days. In fact, one of them went past the twenty-one days and continued for a full forty days. As you will see in chapter 9, not only did her son's cancer go into remission, but the financial hindrances she had battled in her life also were supernaturally broken.

Why weren't these people satisfied to fast just until they saw the breakthrough they needed in their lives? Fasting is not just a physical discipline; it can be a spiritual feast. Once you "taste and see that the LORD is good" (Ps. 34:8), your hunger for more of His presence eclipses the limitation of your understanding. God knows more about what you need than you do. All the fasts in the Bible—whether one day or forty days—brought reward. But there is something very significant about the number forty throughout Scripture, especially as it applies to fasting.

A few years ago, I was reading through a book someone gave me titled *Prophetic Whisper* by Richard Gazowsky. It is an interesting look at his journey to follow the Lord's call to build Christian TV networks.

Early in the book, he talks about an event that really got my attention.

Mr. Gazowsky and his wife were in a season of fasting and were praying on a beach in California. His wife had apparently walked a little farther down the beach and began praying for a woman they knew who was being tempted into adultery. The moment she spoke the woman's name out loud, "a swarm of flies ascended from the ocean surface, as if orchestrated by an invisible conductor, and swept like a blanket across the water and onto the beach."[1] He rushed over to see if his wife was OK. When she told him she'd been praying for their friend, the Lord revealed what Gazowsky referred to as a "vulnerability in Satan's kingdom," that being the flies.[2]

When I read that, I immediately thought of Matthew 12:24, "Now when the Pharisees heard it they said, 'This fellow does not cast out demons except by Beelzebub, the ruler of the demons.'" They were accusing Jesus of operating with the power of Satan, or as they called him, Beelzebub, which means, "lord of the flies." How interesting that during prayer for someone being tempted by demons, a horde of flies came out of nowhere and descended on this woman.

As Gazowsky found, the "weakness" relates to the life span of flies. You can study just about any of the species and you'll find their reproductive cycles can range from a day to as many as forty days. That is why, in order to exterminate an infestation of flies from a crop, for example, you have to spray pesticides for forty consecutive days in order to utterly destroy them. If you stop short of the full forty days, you will destroy only the existing generation, but the next generation will live on. Just as spraying pesticides for a full forty days wipes out an infestation of flies, when we enter into a season of forty days of fasting and prayer, we can break free of the bondages in our own lives and in the lives of the next generation. As Gazowsky noted, "The devil is a short-term skirmisher."[3]

> "The ruler of this world is coming, and he has nothing in Me."

Jesus didn't fast twenty-five days or even thirty-eight days. "He was there in the wilderness forty days, tempted by Satan, and was with the wild beasts; and the angels ministered to Him" (Mark 1:13).

Later, as Jesus's crucifixion drew closer, He spoke directly to His disciples, sharing with them things that were to come. He said, "I will no longer talk much with you, for the ruler of this world is coming, and he has nothing in Me" (John 14:30). Satan was considered the "ruler of this world," having usurped Adam's authority. But he had nothing in Jesus. Jesus defeated him long before, when He did not fall for any of the devil's temptations in the desert.

Some of you may have been battling with the same pesky sins, or worse, you may be trapped in bondages that you have tried to eradicate, only to have them come back time after time. Maybe you've lived free from the effects of some of those sins but you are seeing the cycle repeated in your children. It is going to take more than a flyswatter to wipe out an infestation of Beelzebub's minions.

The Significance of Forty

Throughout the Bible, the number forty represents cleansing and purifying. The flood in Noah's time took forty days to cleanse the earth of wickedness. Moses's life could be divided up into three different seasons of forty: he spent forty years in Egypt, forty years in the desert, and forty years delivering and bringing the people of God to the Promised Land. He also fasted for forty days on two occasions: the first time while receiving the Law of God in the form of the Ten Commandments, and the second time interceding for the sin of the people.

When Jonah was sent to Nineveh, he gave the inhabitants of that city forty days to repent or expect judgment. The Bible records, "So the people of Nineveh believed God, proclaimed a fast, and put on sackcloth, from the greatest to the least of them" (Jon. 3:5). The king called for the entire land to fast, saying, "Let neither man nor beast, herd nor flock, taste anything; do not let them eat, or drink water. But let man and beast be covered with sackcloth, and cry mightily to God; yes, let every one turn from his evil way and from the violence that is in his hands. Who can tell if God will turn and relent, and turn away from His fierce anger, so that we may not perish?" (vv. 7–9). Their humility, repentance, and worship were seen by God, and they were rewarded with mercy instead of judgment.

> There is a prophetic release that occurs
> in a church or an individual who
> fasts continually for forty days.

After defeating four hundred fifty prophets of Baal and ordering their execution, Elijah fled to the desert to escape the deadly threats of Jezebel. God sent an angel to feed him and watch over him as he rested. When he had eaten the meal the angel prepared for him, he went the next forty days without food. During that time, he spoke with God and received new direction. His insecurities and doubts were removed, and the oppression of the enemy was broken.

But there's more. The word Elijah received during that forty-day fast affected even the next generation. He followed God's instruction to anoint Jehu, Elisha, and others to finish the work, and Jehu is credited with the utter destruction of the woman Jezebel. As the account goes, those who went to bury her body after she was thrown from the tower found only her skull, her feet, and the palms of her hands. They reported to Jehu, "This is the word of the LORD, which He spoke by His servant Elijah the Tishbite, saying, 'On the plot of ground at Jezreel dogs shall eat the flesh of Jezebel; and the corpse of Jezebel shall be as refuse on the surface of the field, in the plot at Jezreel, so that they shall not say, "Here lies Jezebel"'" (2 Kings 9:36–37).

Flies represent demons in the Word, as do other animals. If you could see into the spirit world, many demons resemble animals. For example, the Bible said that when the seed of God's Word is sown, the birds of the air come to eat it up (Matt. 13:4, 19). When Jesus said, "They will take up serpents" (Mark 16:18), He was referring to demonic powers. The Bible talks about treading on snakes and scorpions (Luke 10:19). David, in foretelling Jesus's experience on the cross, said, "Strong bulls of Bashan have encircled me" (Ps. 22:12). Those spirits came at Him, goring Him like bulls.

> Devils will start—you guessed it—
> dropping like flies!

These demon spirits attach themselves to our lives as generational curses, bondages, strongholds of the mind, lust, perversion, and addictions of every kind.

The problem with most churches is that we just swat at the flies for a few days when they are right up in our faces. They go away for a while, but they keep coming back. It's time to clean house! It's time for a scriptural season of cleansing. Devils will start—you guessed it—dropping like flies, not only those in your life and your generation, but also the future generation of demons that would be passed down to your children.

Solomon wrote, "Dead flies putrefy the perfumer's ointment, and cause it to give off a foul odor" (Eccles. 10:1). Flies would get into the special anointing oil. They'd get stuck in it, die, and spoil the fragrance. Flies hinder the anointing in your life. Your worship gets polluted by flies of lust and perversion. We are supposed to walk in that pure anointing that pierces hearts, breaks yokes, delivers from bondages, and heals the sick. It's time to get rid of the "flies" in your business, your marriage, your mind, your house. They cannot stand the power of the Holy Ghost and the intimacy of the presence of Jesus that comes from forty days of bombarding heaven.

Some might say, "But forty days is a long time!" Is it really? I read an article in our local paper about the Muslim celebration of Ramadan, when all

Muslims—old, young, even children—fast from sunrise to sunset for thirty days. At the end of each of those days, they all come together to break the fast and pray to their god, Allah. It is a form of worship for them, helping them focus on spiritual things instead of earthly needs. They come together all over the world for this thirty-day religious event, sacrificing and praying to a god who isn't even alive; his bones are still in the grave. Did you know that Islam is the fastest-growing religion in the United States? It is anticipated that in a few years, one in four worldwide will be converted to Islam.

> His rewards are waiting to be released,
> so what are we waiting for?

The scandals and corruption on the front pages of our newspapers and the gross perversion that is prevalent on every level of society tell us how much we need revival in this country. How much more should we, as Christians, devote ourselves to fasting and prayer? God promised, "If My people who are called by My name will humble themselves, and pray and seek My face, and turn from their wicked ways, then I will hear from heaven, and will forgive their sin and heal their land" (2 Chron. 7:14). God does not lie. His promises are true; His rewards are waiting to be released, so what are we waiting for? It doesn't matter how dark the hour is or what is going on in the White House or overseas. God rules and reigns above all those things.

Take Daniel's fast as an example. For three weeks he said he "ate no pleasant food" (Dan. 10:3). Generally, "pleasant food" is thought to mean more festive foods, such as sweets and the like. That may not sound like much of a sacrifice until you think about the fact that we're addicted to sugar! According to Dr. Colbert's research, Americans consume roughly 11,250 pounds of sugar in a lifetime![4] If you fasted from just sweets for forty days, you would rid your body of many toxins and probably shed several pounds. For some of you, it would be a major sacrifice!

Daniel also drank no wine. As a believer in this day and time, that certainly should not be a problem. But then he said he ate no flesh, or meat. That is going to hit a lot of folks hard!

No soft drinks, candy bars, cookies, cakes, sugar-coated cereals (yes, sugar is everywhere in our American diet), hot dogs, burgers, steaks, beef tacos, barbequed ribs, ham biscuits…I could go on and on.

But God sees that sacrifice. When you go out with people at the office to a steakhouse and you choose to have the garden salad, baked potato (no Bacon Bits), and ice water instead of that medium-well, 24-ounce T-bone steak, God takes notice. You're cleansing, you're purifying, and you're destroying flies!

> **Can you forgo that Snickers bar in the afternoon to be delivered from a recurring sin?**

Can you forgo that Snickers bar in the afternoon to be delivered from a recurring sin? To have more of the presence of Jesus in your life, can you drink water instead of sugary, caffeinated drinks for forty days? Do you want to do more than just swat at those flies of doubt and confusion that inundate your thoughts?

Like Jesus told the disciples at the well in Samaria, when you open yourself to know the will of the Father and do the will of the Father, no steak or cake compares. Nothing can fill you and satisfy you like that. Get ready for the presence of Jesus like you have never had before.

If I were hungry, I would not tell you; for the world is Mine, and all its fullness. Will I eat the flesh of bulls, or drink the blood of goats? Offer to God thanksgiving, and pay your vows to the Most High. Call upon Me in the day of trouble; I will deliver you, and you shall glorify Me.

—PSALM 50:12–15

Chapter 6

God's Coming to Dinner?

If we are not careful, we can allow life to get us into the same old ruts and routines without even realizing it. Our relationship with the Lord can suffer the same fate. When we don't do what it takes to stay sharp and sensitive to the Holy Spirit, our praise, worship, offerings, and even preaching can become heartless routines to God. As a believer, you can pray, read your Bible, and go to church week after week and still be losing sight of your first love. It is not that you don't love the Lord, but the business of life can bring you to the point of losing your freshness, your enthusiasm, and your sensitivity to His Spirit and what pleases Him.

> I can just hear our heavenly Father
> sighing, "Religion again?"

My mother was an excellent cook. But if she had gotten so caught up in other things that all she ever put on the table for us was meat loaf every night of the week, I don't think it would have taken long for me to find somewhere else to eat. The disappointing sound of comments like, "Aw, Mom, meat loaf again?" would have been common at my house. What if God were hungry and all we have to feed Him is our same dull religious routines day after day? Just like ending up with meat loaf on the table every night, I can just hear our heavenly Father sighing, "Religion again?"

Out of the Religion Box

That's why God said to Israel, "If I were hungry, I would not tell you; for the world is Mine, and all its fullness" (Ps. 50:12). God owns the cattle on a thousand hills. He does not need our routines. He does not savor heartless activity. He does not want our "leftovers" when He can get "fed" elsewhere. True worship that comes from our hearts feeds Him and satisfies Him; it is something He desires—and deserves. Our religiosity of going through the motions once a week does not please Him as much as our obedience to His Word.

The reason this subject fits in a book about fasting is simple: fasting is a constant means of renewing yourself spiritually. The discipline of fasting breaks you out of the world's routine. It is a form of worship—offering your body to God as a living sacrifice is holy and pleasing to God (Rom. 12:1). The discipline of fasting will humble you, remind you of your dependency on God, and bring you back to your first love. It causes the roots of your relationship with Jesus to go deeper.

God desires to move powerfully in your life. His plans for you are always progressing and developing. He desires to speak to you, as one would speak to a friend. That's how He spoke with Abraham. When God came to judge the wickedness of Sodom and Gomorrah, He stopped by Abraham's tent on the way. Can you imagine looking outside one day and seeing the Lord walking up to your front door with two angels? Talk about out of the ordinary! Abraham rushed to meet the Lord and bowed low to worship

Him. He asked the three visitors to tarry so he could bring water to wash their feet and prepare a meal. The three welcomed his invitation and stayed.

> Fasting is a constant means of renewing yourself spiritually.

Abraham was a man who worshiped God, who spoke with God, and who had followed God's call to leave everything and follow Him to a land that He would show him. His worship and faithfulness had fed God for many years, and suddenly he had the opportunity to feed Him in the natural sense. When you feed God, He will tell you things that He may hide from others. The Bible says that after they ate, God told Abraham he and Sarah would have a son in a year. He even shared with Abraham His plans for Sodom and Gomorrah. Notice, too, that Abraham was then in a very intimate place with God in which he could intercede on behalf of the righteous who might be found in those wicked cities.

There are dimensions of our glorious King that will never be revealed to the casual, disinterested worshiper.

There are walls of intercession that will never be scaled by dispassionate religious service. But when you take steps to break out of the ordinary and worship Him as He deserves, you will begin to see facets of His being you never knew existed. He will begin to share secrets with you about Himself, His plans, His desires for you. When you worship God as He deserves, He is magnified.

David was a man after God's heart. He was a man who fasted often, and not just from food. As a youth, he was often in the fields alone with just the sheep and his God. After he was anointed king, he spent many days running for his life. David wrote Psalm 34 while alone and on the run from Saul in the land of the Philistines. But David stirred himself to worship God even in those conditions, proclaiming, "His praise shall continually be in my mouth" (v. 1), and "Taste and see that the LORD is good" (v. 8). A routine worshiper in those circumstances would have been totally overwhelmed. But David knew that to worship God was to magnify God. His invitation to all of us to "magnify the LORD with me" (v. 3) still stands open today.

When I was a kid, we didn't have toys like Play-Station and Nintendo. We just had real simple toys and great imaginations. One of the best gifts my parents ever gave me was a big, handheld magnifying glass. To a six- or seven-year-old boy, a magnifying glass is adventure waiting to happen! If I lined it up just right with the light of the sun, I could concentrate the heat from that light and burn a hole in a piece of trash, or even toast an unsuspecting ant. And, of course, there was the main feature: the ability to enlarge anything you wanted to see. When I held that glass up to an object, I could look at aspects of it that couldn't possibly be seen with normal vision. Magnification didn't make that object any bigger than it actually was, but it greatly enlarged my view, allowing me to see details that were hidden without magnification.

David was calling us to worship the Lord with him. When you worship, you magnify God. Your enemies or circumstances may seem to be so large and so powerful that they are all you can see. But when you worship, you not only magnify God, but you also reduce the size and power of everything else around you. Later in Psalm 34, David said, "I sought the Lord, and He heard me, and delivered me from all my fears" (v. 4). God will hear you when you set your heart to worship Him. When you magnify the Lord, you shrink the supposed power of your enemy, the devil. The greatest thing you can do in the midst of a battle is magnify the Lord. Jehoshaphat is proof of that. When under attack, the whole nation cried out, fasted, and worshiped God. Jehoshaphat sent the praisers out ahead of the army to magnify their God, and He utterly delivered Judah from their enemy.

When Jesus spoke with the woman at the well in Samaria, His words set her free. She had been married many times and was living with a man who was not her husband. Her relatives had routinely worshiped in Samaria but had been told they were to worship in Jerusalem. At Jacob's Well, Jesus taught her that the "true worshipers will worship the Father in spirit and truth; for the Father is seeking such to worship Him" (John 4:23). With everything else He said to her, she knew she had found the Messiah, or at least He had found her. So she ran back to town, telling everyone, "Come, see a Man who told me all things that I ever did" (v. 29). The Bible says the town came out to see and hear Him—to worship Him.

> When you worship, you magnify God.

In the meantime, His disciples returned with food, but He told them He was not hungry. He said, "I have food to eat of which you do not know....My food is to do the will of Him who sent Me, and to finish His work" (vv. 32, 34.) The worship of that woman had so satisfied Jesus that He was no longer hungry for natural food. The disciples were busy gathering food, but she took time to worship and feed Him that which He most desired.

What is God saying about you? Is it, "Religion again?" Or does He dine with you, fellowship with you, and share with you deep secrets and plans for the future? Whatever you may be facing or going through right now, I want you to heed David's call to magnify the Lord. If you are in a rut or a routine where your worship just isn't cutting it, if you have not heard God speak to you in a long time, if your circumstances seem to be the biggest obstacle in your life, stop everything and begin a fast. One day, several days, some food, all food—the details are not as important as your heart's desire to satisfy God with your worship and sacrifice.

It is written, "Man shall not live by bread alone, but by every word that proceeds from the mouth of God."

—Matthew 4:4

Chapter 7

You Shall Be Filled

Our American diets are loaded with sugars, toxins, processed foods, meats, etc. Yet it is possible for us to be eating large meals, be overweight, and *still* be malnourished. In Colbert's book *Toxic Relief*, he states, "We may be actually starving from a nutritional standpoint, while at the same time becoming grossly obese.... Sadly, we really are digging our graves with our forks and knives!"[1]

In that sense, it is easy to see how our physical lives again parallel our spiritual lives. We can become overnourished on a hefty diet of church programs and activities, religious structure, and traditions of men and yet be severely undernourished when it comes to the deeper things of God. Do you know what Dr. Colbert refers to as the "single most effective answer to overnourishment"? Fasting. He has found that "more than anything else, fasting is a dynamic key to cleansing your body from a lifetime collection of toxins, reversing overnourishment and the diseases it brings and ensuring a wonderful future of renewed energy, vitality, longevity, and blessed health."[2]

> **When you hunger for God, He will fill you.**

Jesus said, "Blessed are those who hunger and thirst for righteousness, for they shall be filled" (Matt. 5:6). When you begin to develop a hunger for the deeper things of God, He will fill you. However, sometimes just being in a good service is not enough. I believe God is already raising up people in this hour who do not want a diet of just "church as normal" any longer. I see it at Free Chapel; people are fasting and developing a hunger for more of God, and religious traditions are having to just get out of the way. Hungry people are desperate people. They will push over the custom; they will push over the ritual—they don't want to leave hungry.

Hungry in Flesh...Hungry in Spirit

Jesus found such hunger while visiting Tyre and Sidon. A woman whose daughter was possessed and tormented by a devil heard that He was there. But the woman was Greek, "a Syro-Phoenician by birth" (Mark 7:26), and, therefore, outside of the covenant God had made with Israel. But that didn't matter to her. She was hungry, and her faith was persistent. Even when Jesus discouraged her, saying that the "bread" was first for the children of Israel, she was hungry enough to ask for even a crumb that would fall to the floor. Many of the children who sat at the table had not shown such great hunger. Jesus honored her request, and her daughter was healed because of her persistence (vv. 29–30).

Hungry people are desperate people, and they are hungry for more of God than they have ever had. They are breaking out of religious rules, regulations, and traditional thinking and breaking through to more of His presence, more of His power to turn situations around, more of His healing power, and more of His miracle-working power! Only Jesus satisfies that hunger!

When you hunger for more,
you will receive more.

It was such hunger that was stirred in the heart of a Gentile centurion in Caesarea who fasted, prayed to God always, and gave generously to the poor. Though they were Gentiles, Cornelius and his household devoutly feared and served God. As Cornelius was fasting and praying one day, like Daniel, an angel appeared to him with a message. The angel said, "Your prayers and your alms have come up for a memorial before God" (Acts 10:4). And then the angel instructed him to send for Peter, who was nearby in Joppa. Peter, who was fasting at the time as well, saw a vision from God in which many foods that were unlawful for Jews to eat were presented to him. He was still puzzled by the vision when Cornelius's messengers arrived. Going with them to his house the next day and hearing of the hunger in this man's heart, Peter understood that the vision meant that the gospel was not to be withheld from the Gentiles. As he shared the gospel with those of Cornelius's household, the Holy Spirit fell and baptized them all, and later they were baptized in water. (See Acts 10.)

Fasting stirs a hunger in your spirit that goes deeper than the temporary hunger you experience in your flesh. When you hunger for God, He will fill you. Jesus went through cities where He could do no miracles—because there was no hunger. As Jesus entered Capernaum, He was confronted by a Roman centurion whose servant was paralyzed and tormented (Matt. 8:5–13). But the centurion knew it would take only a word from Jesus for the servant to be healed. When he said those words to Jesus, the Bible says Jesus was amazed at his faith and told those around him, "I have not found such great faith, not even in Israel!" (v. 10). He was saying, "So many in Abraham's lineage don't have the hunger this man has shown. They come to see Me, but they don't hunger." In this day, God is saying, "I'm looking for somebody who wants something. I'm looking for somebody who will do more than show up, but they will hunger for that which I want to place in them!"

God honors what others call "unlawful" hunger. Matthew 12:1–8 tells of a time when Jesus and the disciples were walking and talking together. The disciples became hungry, and as they walked, they "began to pluck heads of grain and to eat" (v. 1). But it was unlawful to "pick grain" on the day of rest. That day you were not to labor for yourself but be devoted to the Lord. So when the Pharisees noticed what the disciples were doing, they said, "Your disciples are doing what is not lawful to do on the Sabbath!" (v. 2). But they were walking and talking with the Lord of the Sabbath! So Jesus said to the Pharisees, "Have you not read what David did when he was hungry, he and those who were with him: how he entered the house of God and ate the showbread which was not lawful for him to eat, nor for those who were with him, but only for the priests? . . . Yet I say to you that in this place there is One greater than the temple. But if you had known what this means, 'I desire mercy and not sacrifice,' you would not have condemned the guiltless. For the Son of Man is Lord even of the Sabbath" (vv. 3–4, 6–8).

The Pharisees couldn't move past their own traditions to recognize that the Bread of Life stood before them. They were satisfied with their own religion and did not hunger. But when you hunger for more, you will receive more. God will break all the religious rules for you. Perhaps someone has told you, "With your background, God can't use you," or "Because you're a woman, you can't preach," or "You don't have the right 'connections' to do what you want to do." When you hunger for God, He will break the rules of man and cause His favor to come on your life.

Anybody can be normal. Normal is overrated. Someone has to say, "But I want more! Lord, I'm hungry! I'm going to have to push tradition aside! I'm going to have to push religious rules aside! I'm going to have to push all of the rituals aside because I'm starving to death, and I just can't do 'church as usual' any longer." My suggestion is to begin by pushing the plate aside. Show God that you are serious. We must get to the place where we are desperate for God again. We must begin to desire Him more than food or drink. Let us be filled with the Bread of Life instead of the refuse of religion. Begin to make fasting a regular discipline, and see how God answers your hunger!

Do not be afraid, Abram. I am your shield,
your exceedingly great reward.

—Genesis 15:1

Chapter 8

Rewarded Openly

God said, "Let the priests, who minister to the Lord, weep between the porch and the altar" (Joel 2:17). On a house, the "porch" is the part everybody can see; it represents the more public aspects of your ministry. The altar represents private ministry. In the life of a believer, there should always be more private than public ministry to God. When you read about Jesus, you do not see Him praying in public nearly as much as you see Him praying in private. The Bible says He would often pray through the night and have intimate times alone with His Father. Out of those times in private devotion, public demonstrations of God's power would be poured forth in healings, raising of the dead, abundance, and more. Victories are not won in public but in private. That is why fasting, whether corporately or individually, is a private discipline. Where there is little private discipline, there is little public reward.

Keep It Personal

Earlier I showed you how in Matthew chapter 6, Jesus detailed the three duties of a Christian: giving, praying, and fasting. There is something else I want you to see in that chapter. Jesus said, "Take heed that you do not do your charitable deeds before men, to be seen by them. Otherwise you have no reward from your Father in heaven" (Matt. 6:1). He was talking about public and private ministry. He added, "When you do a charitable deed, do not sound a trumpet before you as the hypocrites do in the synagogues and in the streets, that they may have glory from men. Assuredly, I say to you, they have their reward. But when you do a charitable deed, do not let your left hand know what your right hand is doing, that your charitable deed may be in secret; and your Father who sees in secret will Himself reward you openly" (vv. 2–4).

> **Fasting will break poverty from your life.**

Whether done corporately or individually, fasting is a personal, private discipline. It is a sacrifice born out of expectancy. That is not to imply that fasting is a manipulative tool to get something from God, but a "reasonable service" (Rom. 12:1) that God rewards openly. Remember the hundredfold return? God's rewards are for all to see. Just look at the life of Job. He went through a devastating trial and lost everything. His wealth, his family, and his health were all stripped away. Yet he prayed, he fasted, and he remained faithful to private devotion. Job said, "I have esteemed the words of his mouth more than my necessary food" (Job 23:12, kjv). And God "restored Job's losses" and gave him "twice as much as he had before" (Job 42:10). The Bible also says that He "blessed the latter days of Job more than his beginning" (v. 12) and even gave him more sons and daughters. God's open rewards flooded Job's life.

Now I want to share with you some of the open rewards that God told me He would pour out on us at Free Chapel as we were diligent to seek Him in giving, praying, and fasting. These same rewards are open to every believer!

First, He told me that fasting will break poverty from your life. As I plant a seed each time I fast, major blessings return on my life. Again looking at Joel 2:15–16, the people were so poor and in such a famine that they couldn't even bring an offering. But God said to "blow the trumpet in Zion, sanctify a fast, call a solemn assembly" (KJV). After that fast, the threshing floor was full of wheat, the oil vats were overflowing, and they ate in plenty and were satisfied. The Lord brought great financial blessing to people who fasted and prayed. When fasting is a lifestyle, poverty will not be.

Health and healing will follow fasting.

That does not mean that you can fast soft drinks for one day and fall into wealth. But if you begin to fast on a regular basis, and you begin to honor God with fasting, prayer, and giving, you will see for yourself that it is directly linked to poverty being removed from your life. It is interesting that the three wisest men in the Old Testament—Joseph, Daniel, and Solomon—were also the three wealthiest men! Joseph was forced to fast in prison. According to history, only the prisoner's family members were allowed to bring them food, and his family was in another country. But after that season of his life, Joseph became fabulously wealthy and was put over all the money of Egypt (Gen. 41:39–45). Solomon humbled himself in fasting and in prayer, and God greatly increased his wealth and wisdom (1 Kings 3:10–13). Likewise, Daniel, who diligently sought God through fasting and prayer while in Babylonian captivity, was given wisdom over all the others and greatly prospered in the days of Darius the king (Dan. 6:1–4).

God also said that health and healing would follow fasting. Of His chosen fast God said, "Then your light shall break forth like the morning, your healing shall spring forth speedily" (Isa. 58:8). Fasting humbles you and brings clarity, even allowing you to get unforgiveness and bitterness out of your heart. Some people have tried and tried to truly forgive someone but have never been able to let the matter go. Begin a fast, and trust God to work that in your heart. Earlier in the book, I told you how fasting helps you physically because it cleanses your body and gives your organs time to rest. It also helps you "spring clean" in a spiritual sense because it makes you sensitive to the desires of the Lord. Unforgiveness, bitterness, and the like can all be linked to illnesses, fatigue, stress, and more.

> Fasting will also overcome sexual addictions and demonic powers.

When we've been preparing for our annual fasts, the Lord has told me to hold miracle services. He said, "I want you to take a half- or full-page ad in the paper. Tell those who are diseased and suffering with AIDS, leukemia, heart disease, and other things that there is a church that has been fasting and seeking God for healing." When you fast and pray, you should *expect* miracles to follow.

Fasting will also overcome sexual addictions and demonic powers. It will break great sin off people. In Matthew 17:21, Jesus said of that stubborn demon that "this kind does not go out except by prayer and fasting," remember? There's a phenomenal story in the Book of Judges, chapters 19–20, where fasting made the difference in a major battle against a people over-come with sexual perversion. A Levite was traveling with his concubine and stopped in the land of Gibeah, which belonged to the Benjamites. The men of that city had become wicked and delighted in lewd homo-sexual acts (Judg. 19:22).

The men surrounded the house the Levite was vis-iting and demanded that he be sent out so they could "know him carnally." They ended up brutally raping and murdering the man's concubine instead, and she died on the doorstep of the house. When he found her lying there the next morning, he was outraged. He sent pieces of her body with a word to all the tribes of Israel, condemning them for allowing that sort of wickedness to exist in their midst and demanding that they rise up and do something about it.

The armies of Israel gathered against Benjamin. They went out to fight and lost twenty-two thou-sand men the first day (Judg. 20:21). They came back, regrouped, and fought against the Benjamites again, this time losing eighteen thousand (v. 25). Before they went out to fight the third day, God sent the prophet Phinehas with a message to *fast* and pray. So the men fasted for twenty-four hours, and when they went back out against that homosexual spirit, its power was broken and it was defeated (vv. 26–48)!

Now, we don't wrestle with flesh and blood. But there is a spirit behind homosexuality. There is a spirit behind pornography. There is a spirit behind adultery. There is a spirit behind fornication. These demonic spirits of perversion manipulate and use people like puppets on a string. But fasting will break the stronghold of demonic sexual addictions like pornography, homosexuality, adultery, fornication, and lust.

God will also target your children who are being led off and destroyed by the enemy's devices. In the Book of Joel, God called for a holy fast. And He said, "It shall come to pass afterward that I will pour out My Spirit on all flesh; your sons and your daughters shall prophesy" (Joel 2:28). Many times the rewards of fasting come after the fast, though from time to time answers can come during the fast. Look at the story of Hezekiah's son, Manasseh, who became king of Judah (2 Chron. 33:1–13). Manasseh was a wicked king whom God had warned many times to no avail. Then the army of Assyria captured Hezekiah's son, put a hook in his nose, bound him in chains, and took him to Babylon. In his distress, Manasseh cried out to God and humbled himself with fasting. The Bible says God heard his plea and "brought him back to Jerusalem into his kingdom. Then Manasseh knew that the LORD was God" (v. 13).

I have heard so many stories of children who were backslidden and being drawn away by the enemy, as with a hook in their nose. They wound up bound to pornography and trapped by drugs, alcohol, and every sort of addiction. Maybe you have rebellious children or sons and daughters who are committing fornication, but I'm telling you, fasting and praying will absolutely break those spirits off their lives.

> ### God will also target your children.

I received this letter from Shauna, a member of our congregation, about her son. She wrote:

> My son was a born-again, Holy Ghost–filled fifteen-year-old when his dad committed suicide. He turned his back on God and ran from Him for the past fifteen years, but God never gave up on him! He and his brand-new wife came to service after their wedding in

Tennessee. They sat in the balcony. When you gave the altar call, you wouldn't give up. You said, "The Holy Spirit won't let me stop. He says there is someone here that if you don't take this opportunity today, you will never get another one." My son said he looked up and you were pointing right at him. He looked over at his new wife and said, "Well, are we going?" Both of them came down and accepted Jesus as their Lord and Savior. His new wife was raised Buddhist and had never heard about Jesus until she met my son. Thank you for not letting "time" get in the way of one more salvation! My fast ended January 22, and ten days later two of my requests were answered!

"Your Father...will Himself reward you openly" (Matt. 6:4). God does not lie. He has spoken to me that He will bring in souls during our annual fasts, and we have seen the fruit of that reward as well. The thirty-fold, sixtyfold, and hundredfold returns are available in the life of every believer. God is no respecter of persons. What He has done in our church, in the lives of our members, He will do for you when you set your heart to seek Him through fasting.

I will praise the name of God with a song, and will magnify Him with thanksgiving. This also shall please the LORD better than an ox or bull, which has horns and hooves. The humble shall see this and be glad; and you who seek God, your hearts shall live.

—PSALM 69:30–32

Chapter 9

Nothing Shall Be Impossible—It Works!

I could tell you more and more of what God will do when you fast, but the testimonies of people from Free Chapel who participate in our yearly fast say it all. My heart is overwhelmed every year when we begin hearing the testimonies of healings, financial blessings, lost children being brought home, and more.

Stories of Hope

Susan had worked at a one company for fifteen years but lost her job when they were bought out by another company. Making matters more overwhelming, in December, Susan's thirty-five-year-old brother died suddenly, leaving her deeply grieved and broken-hearted. She found the grace to join the fast with the church at the beginning of the year. To her amazement, the company contacted her in March and said, "We're going to give you a year's salary and extended benefits for a full year." With that money, she and her husband became debt free, except for their home, and were able to purchase a newer vehicle. She later told us that, as a result of the fast, God had restored her desire to live.

Darren and his wife, Sarah, were told that they could not have any children. They went on the twenty-one-day fast. Later that year, he testified, "The devil tried to destroy the Lord's blessing, but we have a baby in our arms this year that we didn't have this time last year!"

I received a note from Joan, another of our members, who wrote, "My husband took the challenge of the twenty-one-day fast, even though he was not yet saved. Fourteen days into the fast, he woke up in the middle of the night crying. The next morning, he gave his life to Christ and was baptized in the Holy Ghost that night! Not only did my husband get saved on a twenty-one-day fast, but on February 13, my husband

and all of our children, even my sister-in-law, were baptized. To God be the glory!"

Lisa and her son, Ben, used to attend Free Chapel. Life came to a jolting halt for them at one point after Ben was diagnosed with leukemia. He had gone through chemotherapy and had all the side effects. On January 5, the first Sunday in January when we began the fast, Ben was lying in the Intensive Care Unit, literally fighting for his life with a 107-degree fever. I knew the severity of the situation, so I proclaimed that we would begin that fast for Ben's recovery. Lisa told me Ben awoke at that same moment—the fever broke, he suffered no brain damage, and the leukemia went into total remission.

But Lisa's story doesn't stop there. She joined the twenty-one-day fast that year and continued on it for a full forty days. This mother, in financial crisis, with a son near death and suffering from leukemia, fasted for forty days. God honors that kind of faith and devotion. The Holy Spirit spoke to a man and his wife in our church to buy Lisa a brand-new van. I called her and asked if she could come by the church office, but I didn't tell her anything further. On her way, the car she was driving at the time broke down! She finally arrived, terribly apologetic, having no idea what was about to happen. I handed her the keys to a beautiful new van complete with a DVD player for Ben to enjoy—and a check for an extra five thousand dollars that the couple wanted her to have!

Several weeks later, I called her up on the platform, and we shared her testimony. Earlier that morning, I asked her how much debt she was in. She said she only owed twenty thousand dollars on her house because she had paid off all her other debts with the prior five-thousand-dollar gift. In that morning service, I presented her with another check from that same couple, this time for twenty-five thousand dollars. Lisa and her son had lived their last year in poverty, thanks to a debt-free future, the open reward that God poured out on their sacrificial obedience.

One year, only three days into the fast, Melissa testified that her father had been battling prostate cancer and that she had begun the fast on his behalf. When he went to the doctors for a procedure, to their shock, the doctors found no signs of the cancer anywhere! God healed him. What I loved about her testimony was that she did not stop after the three days. She said, "I'm going longer to see what else God wants to do."

God is no respecter of persons. His delight is to reward His children. He is honored and magnified when we are willing to seek Him at all costs.

Fasting will bring your life and your ministry to others out of obscurity. One Sunday, Steve testified that he had gone on to fast the full forty days. He said:

> I have a ministry where I go into prisons and jails full-time. But I'll be honest with you; I'm a preacher, and I'm filled with the Holy Spirit, but God told me I had a spirit of gluttony on me. That is why I began this fast. I didn't ask for God to open doors; I told God I was sick of the spirit of gluttony cheating me out of the spiritual things God had for my life and locking doors and locking finances and locking everything else that God has for me.

This brother started seeing more doors open for him than he could even handle. He began getting invitations to share at other prisons and to be interviewed by TV stations—he was even interviewed by a policeman who used to arrest him before Steve gave his life to the Lord.

The Lord has assured me over the years that fasting will bring in the lost. Cheryl told us about her twenty-nine-year-old unsaved cousin, Debbie, who called her out of the blue during the annual fast. She was troubled and wanted to get together with Cheryl, saying, "We don't have to eat or anything. I just need to talk with you." Debbie began to share with Cheryl about problems she was having with her marriage and more. Cheryl told her, "The best thing you can do, Debbie, is to find a relationship with Jesus for yourself. I don't know if you've ever prayed or accepted Him, but I can't leave here today without asking if you have ever been saved." Debbie willingly prayed with her cousin and accepted Christ for the first time in her life!

> The Lord has assured me over the years that fasting will bring in the lost.

Fasting makes you more sensitive to the timing and voice of the Holy Spirit. Even in the middle of the fast, Cheryl had a boldness that she typically might not have had. Fasting does such a work in your life that the lost are often drawn to you and to what God is doing. It's not that we manipulate God through our works, forcing His hand. Fasting simply breaks you and brings your faith to a new level.

By this point, I hope that I have been able to clear up the misconceptions about what fasting is—and what it is not—and why it is a discipline that should not be missing in the life of any believer. It is a vital part of that threefold cord of normal Christian duties that Jesus outlined in Matthew 6: giving, praying, and fasting. It cleanses your body and promotes health in many practical ways. It brings you into a deeper relationship with the Lord than can be enjoyed through routine religion. Don't wait for a good time. As God pointed out, there just isn't one. You are not too young or too old. After all, Anna was a prophetess who was in her eighties when she worshiped day and night, fasting and praying (Luke 2:37).

As I mentioned earlier, if Jesus could have received what He needed to walk out His ministry here on Earth—without fasting—He would not have fasted. But He did fast; in fact, He has continued fasting for us for over two thousand years. During His last meal with the disciples, He gave them the cup and said, "I will not drink of this fruit of the vine from now on until that day when I drink it new with you in My Father's kingdom" (Matt. 26:29). I have seen people who have never fasted before experience marvelous breakthroughs in their lives. If you are ready to bring supernatural blessings into your life and release the power of God to overcome any situation, begin today making the discipline of fasting a part of your life. You will be greatly rewarded!

Section 2

Opening a Door to God's Promises

When the woman saw that the fruit of the tree was good for food...

—GENESIS 3:6, NIV

Why Is It So Hard?

It is still amazing to me that food was the entice-ment used to cause Adam and Eve to sin, resulting in the fall of mankind. I find it equally interesting that Jesus began His earthly ministry—to redeem us from sin—by abstaining from food.

I imagine it was an extraordinary sight for John the Baptist to see his own cousin, the Lamb of God, descending into the water to be baptized like everyone else. Most of the folks who were baptized that day probably went home afterward to celebrate with a fine feast, talking about what they had seen and heard. Jesus did not. He followed the leading of the Holy Spirit, beginning His earthly ministry alone, fasting for forty days and nights while being tempted in the desert (Matt. 3:16–4:11).

The first thing Jesus felt in His earthly ministry for you and me was hunger. The last thing that He felt on this earth was thirst as the Lord of glory hung dying on a cruel cross, according to John 19:28.

So my question is, why does the body of Christ have such a hard time with the discipline of fasting? Lack of control over the flesh opened the door for sin's temptation in the Garden of Eden, but Jesus took control over His flesh, sanctifying Himself to break the power of temptation. When Jesus fasted for forty days and nights, Satan tempted Him to "command that these stones be made bread" (Matt. 4:3, KJV). The enemy tried repeatedly to cause Jesus to focus on the desire for food rather than on the assignment and the purposes of the Father, but Jesus knew that sanctification is an essential key to opening a door of God's blessings.

If Jesus needed to fast, how much greater is our need to fast? I was eighteen years old when I went on my first complete twenty-one-day fast. It was one of the most difficult things I had ever done. Fasting is never easy. Honestly, I know of nothing more wearisome than fasting. Jesus understands the difficulty of depriving ourselves of food. In Hebrews 4:15 we read, "For we do not have a High Priest who cannot sympathize with our weaknesses, but was in all points tempted as we are, yet without sin." He also provides strength for us to overcome temptation in Hebrews 4:16. "Let us therefore come boldly to the throne of grace, that we may obtain mercy and find grace to help in time of need." With these promises in mind, the process became less unpleasant for me.

When you fast, you abstain from food for spiritual purposes. I have heard people say that they were planning to fast TV or computer games or surfing the Internet. It is good to put those things down for a time of consecration if they are interfering with your prayer life or with your study of God's Word or your ministering to the needs of others, but technically, that is not fasting. Fasting is doing without food for a period of time, which generally causes you to leave the commotion of normal activity. Part of the sacrifice of fasting, seeking God, and studying His Word is that normal activity fades into the background.

There are wrong reasons to fast. You do not fast to obtain merit with God or to get rid of sin. There is only one thing that gives us merit with God and cleanses us of sin—the blood of Jesus. However, fasting will begin to bring to the surface any areas of compromise in your life and make you more aware of any sin in your own life so you can repent.

Fasting is not a Christian diet. You should not fast to lose weight, although weight loss is a normal side effect. Unless you put prayer with your fasting, there is no need to fast. Merely doing without food is just starving. When you fast, you focus on prayer and on God's Word.

Finally, you do not fast so that others will notice you. A fast is not an opportunity to show others how deeply spiritual you are, but an opportunity to focus on the needs of others. The world hunger movement has a program called "Let It Growl," a world hunger and awareness fast. During this fast, when participants feel the hunger pangs rise up and their stomachs begin to growl, they remember that one-third of the people in this world go to bed with that same feeling every night because they have no food.

At the time of this writing, I have been pastoring Free Chapel for just over eighteen years. For much of that time, I fasted privately for twenty-one days at the beginning of each year, but about seven years ago, the Holy Spirit led me to ask the church to join the fast.

God has blessed us in more ways than I could have ever imagined.

I was walking through the airport the other day, and a man stopped me and said, "I know who you are. I am one of those people who fasted with your church last year." When you enter into a fast at the beginning of the year with the body of Christ, you link up with thousands of people all over the world who also begin the New Year with a fast. One person fasting is powerful, but when a group of people begin to fast, it is multiplied strength! It is multiplied power!

Dr. David Yonggi Cho pastors the largest church in the world in Seoul, South Korea. Seven hundred fifty thousand members go on a twenty-one-day fast every year. He has fifteen hundred teenagers camp out on Prayer Mountain in tents to fast and pray for seven days each year.

You have been deceived if you believe Christians are not supposed to fast. God expects every one of us to fast—not just some of us. In Matthew chapter 6, He names three things that Christians do: "When you pray…" "When you give…" and "When you fast." He didn't say "if" but "when." If you have a time to pray and a time to give, then you should have a time to fast.

Therefore do not worry, saying, "What shall we eat?" or "What shall we drink?" or "What shall we wear?"...For your heavenly Father knows that you need all these things. But seek first the kingdom of God and His righteousness, and all these things shall be added to you.

—MATTHEW 6:31–33

You can always find a reason not to fast, so you have to make up your mind that you are going to do it, and everything else will take care of itself. If you will determine to set apart the first days of the year to fast, you will set the course for the entire coming year, and God will add blessings to your life all year long. Just as you set the course of your day by meeting with God in the first hours, the same is true of dedicating the first days of the year to fasting.

The first section of this book is called "The Private Discipline That Brings Public Reward." The "rewards" that have surfaced in the lives of those attending Free Chapel and beyond over the past few years have been phenomenal. In this second section, I will share some of the deeper teachings the Lord has given me on fasting as we have continued to seek Him in this manner, and I will encourage you with some of the magnificent testimonies of God's faithfulness to His Word.

And all these, having obtained a good testimony through faith, did not receive the promise, God having provided something better for us, that they should not be made perfect apart from us.

—HEBREWS 11:39–40

Chapter 10

He Pleased God

I am more excited about fasting than I have ever been. Don't get me wrong—I enjoy eating! Though I enjoy eating, I cannot say I enjoy watching people as they cut into a big, steaming, juicy steak while I'm crunching on steamed broccoli. I have found that hungering and thirsting for God brings with it a much greater reward than satisfying the temporary hunger I may be experiencing in my body.

Do you remember Anna? Her story only fills a few lines in Luke's Gospel, but I believe God saw much more in the life of this precious saint. She is called a prophetess, and her simple testimony is that she was "a widow of about eighty-four years [of age], who did not depart from the temple, but served God with fastings and prayers night and day" (Luke 2:37). That just goes to show you that you are never too old to fast. Anna had a hunger for God's Word that was greater than her hunger for food, and her faithfulness in fasting prepared her for what was about to happen.

> Hungering for God brings with it a much greater reward than satisfying the temporary hunger in my body.

After Jesus's birth, Joseph and Mary brought their tiny infant boy to the temple to be dedicated as the firstborn Son. I would imagine that young family walked past hundreds of people in the crowded temple that day, but only one man and one faithful woman truly recognized the Messiah. Simeon was the first to rejoice in seeing Jesus. Then Anna saw Him and instantly gave thanks to God. She then began telling all who looked for the redemption of Israel about the tiny baby who was the long-awaited Messiah (Luke 2:38). Imagine that—a new calling on her life at eighty-four years old!

Although fasting doesn't get any easier with age, it does get easier with grace. When the Holy Spirit calls you to fast, He is preparing you for what is ahead.

Fasting requires faith. As Jesus said, "Blessed are they which do hunger and thirst after righteousness: for they shall be filled" (Matt. 5:6, KJV).

Believe God

The eleventh chapter of the Book of Hebrews is often referred to as "the hall of faith," beginning with the words, "Now faith is the substance of things hoped for, the evidence of things not seen" (Heb. 11:1). Some of the most encouraging words in the Bible are found in this book. It is said that after the birth of Seth to Adam and Eve, people began to call on the name of the Lord (Gen. 4:26). Enoch was born many years later, and his life went a step beyond merely calling on the name of the Lord. Thousands of years after his departure from this earth, the writer of the Book of Hebrews said of him: "By faith Enoch was translated that he should not see death; and was not found, because God had translated him: for before his translation he had this testimony, that he pleased God" (Heb. 11:5, KJV).

What was it about Enoch that was different from those before him? What about his life was so pleasing to God? The answer is found in Hebrews:

> But without faith it is impossible to please him: for he that cometh to God must believe that he is, and that he is a rewarder of them that diligently seek him.
>
> —HEBREWS 11:6, KJV

When the Holy Spirit calls you to fast, He is preparing you for what is ahead.

Enoch knew God. Not only that, Genesis 5:22 says that Enoch "walked with God" for three hundred years! Now, if I were to choose what could be said of me, I would want my testimony to be "he pleased God." Notice that Enoch did not try to please people. In fact, Jude records that Enoch prophesied in a manner that would have made him very unpopular with the party crowd (Jude 14–15). Enoch's primary concern was walking in faith, which is what pleases God. According to Hebrews 11:6, it is reasonable to say that Enoch came to God, he believed God, he diligently sought God, and he was rewarded.

If you want to please God, *believe* God. Take Him at His Word. When the apostle Paul was teaching the Corinthians, a knowledge-seeking society, he told them, "We walk by faith, not by sight" (2 Cor. 5:7). Shadrach, Meshach, and Abed-nego walked by faith and not by sight. The three of them joined Daniel in his initial fast from the king's delicacies. Think about what they saw on their way into that furnace. It had been heated seven times hotter than normal. The heat was so intense that it killed the guards standing by the doors. If they had walked by sight, they would have said, "Today we shall surely be ashes." Instead, by faith, they walked on saying, "Our God whom we serve is able to deliver us from the burning fiery furnace, and He will deliver us from your hand, O king" (Dan. 3:17). Faith is the evidence of things unseen.

Hunger for the Word

Where does the kind of faith that enables you to look to God and believe His Word no matter how grave your circumstances may *appear* come from? Your daughter is unsaved and on drugs. Your father lies dying in a hospital bed. You are about to be evicted from the house you rent because it's been sold out from under you. Your marriage of twenty years has come to an end, and the divorce papers have been signed. I could go on and on. These are very real circumstances that have no solution in the natural. Where does such faith come from?

"Faith comes by hearing, and hearing by the word of God" (Rom. 10:17). The Amplified version of this Scripture verse states, "Faith comes by hearing [what is told], and what is heard comes by the preaching [of the message that came from the lips] of Christ (the Messiah Himself)." It is by hearing God's Word, by hearing the preaching of the gospel, that faith increases. There is something about getting in a church where the anointing flows and you hear the Word of God preached. Faith does not come from programs, dynamite worship teams, or being with a group of people who are like you. Faith comes when you hear a man or woman of God preach the Word without compromise to all who will listen. That is the birthplace of faith. If this revelation truly takes hold of your spirit, you will never allow the devil to talk you out of being faithful to God's house.

> **If you want to please God, believe God.**

Too many Christians find that they are malnourished in the Word but well fed on the world, and they live defeated lives as a result. In the introduction to this section, I mentioned how Eve *saw* that the fruit was good for food. God's Word to Adam and Eve was, "In the day that you eat of it you will surely die" (Gen. 2:17). Yet Eve acted on the wisdom of the world that was spoken by the serpent instead of walking away in faith that God's Word was true.

In contrast, as Jesus fasted in the desert, He was tempted by the same voice that had so cunningly whispered to Eve. Yet Jesus responded, "Man shall not live by bread alone, but by every word that proceeds from the mouth of God" (Matt. 4:4). What had Jesus heard just before beginning that time of fasting? "And lo a voice from heaven, saying, This is my beloved Son, in whom I am well pleased" (Matt. 3:17, KJV). The Word of God sustained Him through forty days and nights without food.

How I wish the body of Christ today had that same kind of hunger for God's Word. I would love to see the day when, if a Christian had to, he or she would rather go to church in pajamas than miss *hearing* God's Word! I know that sounds extreme, but we live in extreme times. We need to understand Jesus's words when He said, "Heaven and earth will pass away, but My words will by no means pass away" (Mark 13:31).

What did young David possess in the natural that made him believe he would be successful against the giant Philistine? Nothing! He was small; he was young; he was not yet a soldier—merely a keeper of sheep. Yet, he walked with God, he knew God, and he sought after God. His faith was all he needed to know that Goliath would fall before him just as the lion and bear had fallen. (See 1 Samuel 17:34–35.)

Diligence

We must diligently feed on God's Word. Sometimes the best thing we can possibly do is starve our flesh and feed our spirit through a fast. Fasting helps you separate what you *want* from what you *need*. It causes you to focus on those things that really matter.

Believe me, fasting allows you many opportunities to diligently seek the Lord! You diligently seek Him when everyone else is going out to the movies, drinking sodas, and eating popcorn and you choose to stay home to be with the Lord because you just *have* to hear from Him. Diligently seeking Him through fasting happens in the morning when everyone else gets up and eats bacon, eggs, pancakes, maple syrup, grits, hash browns, and fried sausage and you choose to spend time with God. It comes when you're at work and everyone else is having burgers, fries, and shakes for lunch, but you are having bottled water! Diligence is when you come home from a long, hard day at work, and all you have had all day is water, yet you separate yourself from the dinner table to feed on the Word.

> We walk by faith. We don't stay still, drowning in our misery.

To be diligent is to be persistent. It means to work hard in doing something and refusing to stop. God delivered the Israelites from Pharaoh's slavery. He parted the Red Sea so they could cross on dry ground, but He allowed Pharaoh's army to drown. Still, the children of Israel got out into the wilderness and started complaining. After all He had done for them, they were not diligent about seeking the Lord, and that older generation never entered into His rest, His reward.

Faith is progressive. Faith never gets into a bad situation and says, "I'm just going to sit here and die. It's over." Faith never stands in the desert, having a pity party with everything drying up around it. You walk by faith. You don't stand still, drowning in your misery. When you get in a wilderness, you keep walking; you keep going forward even if you are only making an inch of progress with each step. When you get into battles, you have to keep saying, "I will move forward."

Reward

When a reward is offered for someone's capture, the reward is provided before it is claimed. The money is placed into an account to be held until the offender is captured. God is a rewarder of those who diligently seek Him (Heb. 11:6), which means He has already laid up rewards for you in heaven. In my mind, when reading this scripture, I've always added, "seek Him…and find Him." That is not what it says. The Bible tells us that if we *seek*, we will *find*.

By beginning each year with a season of fasting and praying, we are *seeking* first His kingdom. The testimonies that come during and after the fast are incredible. I want to share some of the "rewards" people have experienced to encourage you in your faith. Often during the services in January, the microphone will be overrun with people testifying to the goodness of God. I will let some of them share with you in their own words:

> I have been fasting for my family and my children to get saved, and I've gone seven days with no food, just liquids. I was trying to decide whether to start on the Daniel fast today or not. Well, I'm not going to debate it any longer because after two years of running from the Lord, my daughter got saved this very morning—and I want more miracles in my family!

Pastor, we were behind on our house payment, facing foreclosure. Friday, my company bought pizza for everybody. I sat in my office and ate tomato soup instead. I got home that afternoon to discover that the bank had rearranged the whole mortgage. We're caught up! We're current! And we don't have a payment until the first of April!

We've been praying for my daughter-in-law for a year and a half. She has recently gone into a drug program from church. She's been on drugs since she was fourteen. She was up here at the altar this morning on her face, crying out to God. It's a miracle. It is a miracle!

I've been attending Free Chapel for three years, but last year my mother told me, "They're starting a fast." I thought, "Twenty-one days? I don't know if I can do that." Then I remembered that when you put God first, the year will be prosperous. At that time, my wife and I had just one car, and we were living in an apartment. Over the course of the year, I got another car. We moved into a house. I'm a musician, and the artist I have worked with just got a deal with one of the biggest labels in the world. So my family and I will be on the fast again this year—and who knows!

My father is in CCU at Northeast Georgia Medical Center. He had a hernia that had enclosed his colon, which basically killed the colon, the bowel and everything. Five times he has been given up for dead. Right now he is off the vital life support. He is breathing on his own. And they're talking about moving him to a room.

Pastor, this week we had a major mess-up in our bank account. Some people had stolen our debit card and some money, and we started bouncing checks. But praise God, we started fasting. You know, God just came down! We got all the money back for the bounced checks, and the bank reimbursed the money that was stolen from us, too.

I want to share this one with you myself. One year, at the end of the twenty-one-day fast, a couple walked up to me and handed me a bundle of official papers. Puzzled, I opened them up to see the word *DISMISSED* stamped in bold black letters. After that, I read the words, "The Superior Court of Gwinnett County, State of Georgia, Final Judgment and Decree of Divorce." The couple standing before me had been struggling in their marriage for a year, but during that fast, the season of setting everything else aside and diligently seeking God, a miracle happened! Unity replaced division, and the divorce was dismissed. The devil thought he'd racked up another statistic for Christian divorces—but God is a rewarder!

The enemy comes to steal, kill, and destroy, but Jesus came that we might have life more abundantly (John 10:10). There are many things that Jesus's death, burial, and resurrection provide for us. While all are available, none are automatic. God is no respecter of persons. He rewards all who diligently seek Him in faith, because faith is what pleases Him.

I will lift up my eyes to the hills—from whence comes my help? My help comes from the LORD, who made heaven and earth. He will not allow your foot to be moved; He who keeps you will not slumber. Behold, He who keeps Israel shall neither slumber nor sleep.

—PSALM 121:1–4

Chapter 11

Garment of Praise

You never forget the feeling of sorrow and loss that occurs when someone close to you dies. I loved my father dearly. When he passed away in 1991, it took me weeks to get beyond the initial impact of grief and mourning. Each day when I awoke, that sense of loss would hit me again as I thought, "My daddy is dead." He was a wonderful father and grandfather. I am thankful that we had the opportunity to make so many wonderful memories together. His life was indeed a celebration. Though I knew Dad was with the Lord, his absence from this life left a void that took awhile to get over.

In Matthew 9, we see the disciples of John the Baptist coming to Jesus to ask, "Why do we and the Pharisees fast often, but Your disciples do not fast?" (v. 14).

Jesus answered, "Can the friends of the bridegroom mourn as long as the bridegroom is with them? But the days will come when the bridegroom will be taken away from them, and then they will fast" (v. 15).

This is not the only time you see the words *mourn* and *fast* used interchangeably in the Bible. The example the Lord gives in this passage makes it clear that fasting is much like mourning. When you are on a fast, you usually do not feel like celebrating. It is a time to press into God, to seek Him, and to forsake the things of the flesh. Within hours of beginning a fast, you may find that food is the first thing on your mind (right before your stomach begins to growl).

Still, I look forward to the corporate fast here at Free Chapel each year because of the rewards that come from the diligence of an entire church seeking God in that manner. Jesus said, "Blessed are those who mourn, for they shall be comforted" (Matt. 5:4). Who is the comforter other than the Holy Spirit? As the prophet Isaiah began his proclamation of the good news in chapter 61, he foretold of the coming of Christ, who came to:

Comfort all who mourn, to console those who mourn in Zion, to give them beauty for ashes, the oil of joy for mourning, the garment of praise for the spirit of heaviness; that they may be called trees of righteousness, the planting of the Lord, that He may be glorified.

—ISAIAH 61:2–3

I believe that as the church learns to fast (mourn) together, we will see God begin to fulfill these promises in many ways. Are there "burnt out" experiences in your life—ugly reminders of past hurts and failed dreams? Don't throw away the ashes. God will give you beauty for ashes. He will give you the anointing of His presence, which is the oil of joy for your mourning.

Fasting Breaks the Spirit of Heaviness

The spirit of heaviness has to do with despondency, depression, and oppression. Sadly, the biggest pitfall in America is the oldest in the world. Americans use drinking, smoking, drugs, medications, overeating, and other harmful behaviors to try to lift the spirit of heaviness. Think about all the commercials you see for weight loss, smoking cures, antidepressants, etc. Seldom do you turn on a television program without being bombarded by drug company commercials.

Instead of looking for more stuff to put *into* our bodies to ease the pain, we should fast and seek the God who gives us a garment of praise for the spirit of heaviness that afflicts so many. Why is it a garment of praise? You will find that you wear depression and oppression like a garment. It shrouds you in darkness and despair. It is a heavy garment that continues to drag you down. It keeps you from lifting your head and from raising your hands in praise to God.

Heaviness drains worship out of your life. Church is depressing unless you learn to worship. I know that is a strange statement, but it is true. There is nothing worse than a Spirit-filled church that loses the garment of praise and picks up the spirit of heaviness. God desires our praise more than our mere church attendance. That is not to say we should forsake assembling together as a corporate body. But our times together, just as our times alone, should be to glorify and praise our awesome, mighty God. Praise pushes back the enemy!

One of my favorite examples of this fact is found in 2 Chronicles. King Jehoshaphat is told "'a great multitude is coming against you from beyond the sea, from Syria; and they are in Hazazon Tamar' (which is En Gedi). And Jehoshaphat feared, and set himself to seek the Lord, and proclaimed a fast throughout all Judah" (2 Chron. 20:2–3).

Now, Jehoshaphat had just gotten the kingdom of Judah in order. Things were going well. No sooner did they start enjoying that peace when they heard that an army—far larger than they could defeat on their own—was already on its way. Jehoshaphat could have died under that spirit of heaviness. The scripture says that he "feared," but he only paused a moment there. He immediately set himself and all the people of Judah to seek the Lord through fasting and prayer. Then he took his place in the assembly of the people and began to praise—proclaiming who God was and all that God had done for them. He ended by saying, "We have no power against this great multitude that is coming against us; nor do we know what to do, but our eyes are upon You" (v. 12). Then they waited.

How many times do we find ourselves saying that same thing: "I don't know what to do. This problem is far too big for me to handle." We must put our eyes on God! The story continues: "Then the Spirit of the LORD came upon Jahaziel...a Levite of the sons of Asaph, in the midst of the assembly" (v. 14). God told them that the battle was not theirs but His. He told them exactly where the enemy would be, but He said, "'You will not need to fight in this battle. Position yourselves, stand still and see the salvation of the LORD, who is with you, O Judah and Jerusalem!' Do not fear or be dismayed; tomorrow go out against them, for the LORD is with you" (v. 17).

I don't know about you, but realizing that the Lord was going to destroy my enemies would be reason enough to shout! And that is just what the people of Judah did. Young and old "stood up to praise the LORD God of Israel with voices loud and high." The next day, they went early to the place the Lord had directed them. Then Jehoshaphat addressed the people again, saying:

> "Hear me, O Judah and you inhabitants of Jerusalem: Believe in the LORD your God, and you shall be established; believe His prophets, and you shall prosper." And when he had

consulted with the people, he appointed those who should sing to the LORD, and who should praise the beauty of holiness, as they went out before the army and were saying: "Praise the LORD, for His mercy endures forever."

—2 CHRONICLES 20:20–21

Now, notice what happened when they began to praise: "The LORD set ambushes against the people of Ammon, Moab, and Mount Seir, who had come against Judah; and they were defeated" (v. 22).

There is power in corporate fasting and power in corporate praise! It creates a river of healing, a river of deliverance and victory, a river of cleansing in the house of God. It is time to exchange ashes for beauty, mourning for joy, and a garment of heaviness for a garment of praise.

What Eating Accomplishes

A friend called me just as we were about to begin the corporate fast. To my surprise he said, "I feel so sorry for you." He actually felt sorry for me because I was about to lay down food for the joy of seeking the Lord for twenty-one days.

I replied, "Don't feel sorry for me. In fact, I feel sorry for you." Then I challenged him: "I'll make a deal with you. Go ahead and eat your food for the next twenty-one days. We will compare notes at the end of the year to see if the food you ate accomplished for you what fasting for the next twenty-one days accomplished for me." As evidenced in Daniel 1:15, eating does not accomplish what fasting does.

> **There is power in corporate fasting and power in corporate praise!**

I am so blessed to be part of a fellowship that seeks God together through fasting. Battles are won and lives are changed as a result of fasting. In fact, a dramatic change came around Christmastime in the life of a young man whom I will call James. We had started that year off with a corporate fast as we now do every year. Many miracles had occurred in the lives of people throughout the year. This particular Friday night, my family and I had attended the Christmas program at Free Chapel and were driving home. The forecast was calling for severe winter weather to hit over the weekend, so my wife, Cherise, asked me to stop by the grocery store to pick up some essentials. It was late, so I pulled up front and left the car running to keep them warm.

I grabbed the milk, bread, and cereal and got in line to check out. I could see my kids watching me through the store windows. That's when I noticed him. A young man had entered the store right behind me and was now in line behind me holding a few cases of beer. I glanced back at him, and our eyes met for a second. At first, I didn't think much about it because I was just there to get milk and cereal. Remember, I had fasted for twenty-one days at the beginning of the year, and fasting makes you more sensitive to the voice of God. Suddenly, in my spirit I heard the Lord say, "Tell him he has great worth to Me."

I looked back at the young man, and he looked at me, and then he walked away. I went through the line and paid for my things, knowing I was supposed to say something to him. I didn't see him as I left, so I walked out to the car. When I opened the door, Cherise and all the girls were saying, "Daddy, Daddy! Look, look,

look!" They showed me the camera they had brought to take pictures of the Christmas drama. But when I looked at the digital screen, they had taken pictures of the guy from the line. I asked, "What's going on?"

My wife and kids had a bird's-eye view of this guy stealing beer and wine from the store. Not only that, they took pictures of him in the act! That's right, the same young man of whom God said, "He has great worth to Me." My heart sank. I had the chance to tell this young man that he had great worth to God, that he didn't have to continue living like he was living— defeated by the enemy and trapped under a spirit of heaviness. I had not obeyed God, and I felt terrible.

I confessed to my family, "The Lord spoke to my heart, but I didn't obey Him." I jumped out of the car and went back into the store. I looked frantically for the guy in the aisles, and one of my girls ran up behind me and said, "Daddy, he went out the other door." My heart sank again. When I walked outside and got in my car, Cherise said, "I know where he went. He went to the next supermarket down the street."

I said, "You think so?"

She said, "I guarantee you he did. He's in a red Camaro."

I said, "Let's go." Thank God for second chances!

We rode down to the next supermarket, and as we cruised through the parking lot, one of the girls said, "There it is! It's the red Camaro!" I immediately parked, jumped out of the car, and ran inside to look for him. I knew just where to look: the beer and wine section! There he was with the cart filled to the top with cases of beer and wine. He had pushed it to the edge of the aisle where he could slip out behind the cash registers and ease on outside with his load.

But that wasn't God's plan for James! I walked right up to him and I said, "You don't know me, and I don't know you, but God wants you to know that you have great worth to Him." He stared at me for a moment and said, "What did you say?" I reached in my pocket, and I had forty dollars. Handing it to him, I said, "I know when I give you this money you're probably going to buy that alcohol with it, but I've got to obey God, and He told me to tell you, sir, you have great worth to Him, and He loves you."

He said, "I can't believe this is happening. Who are you?"

I said, "I'm a preacher."

"Where do you preach?"

"At Free Chapel over on McEver Road."

He started to tremble and said, "Thank you. I can't, you know, I can't quit," pointing to the cart. He said, "I've been in six rehabs, and I can't quit."

Again I told him what God said about him. He backed up a step or two. I asked, "Are you ready to walk out of here and leave it?" He looked at me very seriously and said, "Let's go!" We walked to the parking lot. Now, the girls were all sitting in the car, praying for this guy the whole time that I was talking to him. The guy walked out wiping tears from his eyes. I put my arm around him and said, "You just need to ask Jesus to help you, son. He knows. He understands. He sent me during this Christmas season to tell you, 'You have great worth.'"

Everyone else, including James himself, had said, "You're worthless. You'll never amount to anything. You're a failure. You've wasted your life." But God saw things differently. I prayed with James in that parking lot, and we parted ways. The last thing he told me was, "I'll be at your church, Pastor." I began to pray for him every day. Christmas came and went. New Year's came and went. We were a few days into our corporate fast when I saw James walking toward me one Sunday morning. He had a big smile on his face. He said, "I told you I'd be here." We started our year off with a miracle!

No matter what is going on in your life right now, you can set yourself to fasting and praying to seek the God who sees you as having great worth. Don't believe the lies of the enemy. Don't sink further under the spirit of heaviness. God has a garment of praise for you. His yoke is easy, and His burden is light. As you fast, you will begin to see yourself through His eyes.

That you may have a walk worthy of the Lord, fully pleasing Him, being fruitful in every good work and increasing in the knowledge of God; strengthened with all might, according to His glorious power, for all patience and longsuffering with joy; giving thanks to the Father who has qualified us to be partakers of the inheritance of the saints in the light.

—COLOSSIANS 1:10–12

Chapter 12

Fasting, Faith, and Patience

I don't really remember what grade I was in, but we did an experiment in elementary school that left a lasting impression on me, even into adulthood. The teacher told us to save our milk cartons from lunch for this special event. We were to bring them back to class with us, where we rinsed them out and cut the funny tops off. She then opened a big container of black potting soil, and we scooped some into our cartons. She handed each one of us a big butter bean seed and told us how to plant the seed in the soil by making a small hole with our finger and dropping the seed in. After I pressed the dirt back down into the hole, I watered the seed, taped my name to the box, and set it in the sunny window beside everyone else's.

Every day when that class started, I ran to the window with the others to see what was happening with the seeds. We couldn't see anything until the third day, when a tiny bit of green sprout began to show in some of the boxes. By day six, most of the boxes had green sprouts, and some even had leaves showing—but not mine. For six days I eagerly ran to the window to look at my box; there was nothing but dirt. I watered it like everyone else did. It sat in the same sun that everyone else's did, but no sprout was showing. I wondered if my seed was even still there.

On the seventh day, I couldn't take it any longer. I arrived to class before anyone else and used my finger to dig around in the soil to see if my seed was still in the box. I pulled it out, and sure enough, it had begun to sprout. My teacher walked in about that time. When she saw what I had in my dirty little fingers, she kindly explained that I really should have left it alone and just waited. Since I had pulled my seed out of the soil too soon, I had destroyed my harvest. She was right. All the other seeds grew strong and tall, and before long, they were filled with multiple pods of butter beans— far more than the one seed that was sown.

Don't Dig It Up!

That little childhood experiment has stayed with me for so long because I have learned that we do the same thing in our spiritual lives. We get a word from the Lord—it's just a seed—but it gets planted deep in our hearts: "God is going to bless me. I'm highly favored of the Lord. God sees my need and will provide for me. He will protect my family and save my lost loved ones." The mountains you face seem so big, but you take that tiny seed of faith, plant it into that mountain, and wait.

> Faith and patience must go together.

Before long, impatience sets in. The mountains seem even bigger than they were before, and your seed isn't showing any sprouts—no matter what you do. Other people are being blessed, but nothing is happening in your situation. You begin to think, "Did I really get that word from God?"—like my wondering if my seed was still in the little box. I knew I had planted it and I didn't think anyone had taken it—but surely it must be gone because I couldn't see anything. You end up getting discouraged. You dig your fingers in and pull your seed out too early, destroying the promise.

Likewise, I've heard people say they just couldn't make it past a day or so on a fast because they got discouraged. They listened to their flesh instead of continuing in faith and felt worse than when they started. What happened to walking by faith and not by sight? Faith and *patience* must go together.

When a man brought his son to the disciples to deliver him from seizures, the disciples were not able to help him. So he brought the boy to Jesus, asking the Lord to have mercy on his son. Jesus cast out the demon that tormented the boy, and he was healed. I can imagine how the disciples began to question themselves and each other. Later, they asked Jesus why they could not cast it out. Jesus answered them saying:

> Because you have so little faith. I tell you the truth, if you have faith as small as a mustard seed, you can say to this mountain, "Move from here to there" and it will move. Nothing will be impossible for you.
>
> —MATTHEW 17:20, NIV

What powerful words Jesus gave us! I encourage you to meditate on this scripture for a while and not just pass over it as familiar territory. People facing major obstacles usually believe they need "great faith" to overcome them, but that isn't what Jesus said. He said "nothing" would be impossible to us—not if we had *great faith*—but if we had faith like the smallest seed.

Someone once sent me a mustard seed from Israel. Just to put things into perspective, a butter bean seed is about four hundred times bigger than a mustard seed, but it will yield only a small bush. On the other hand, a common mustard seed is only about one millimeter in diameter, and it grows into a small tree. The more common mustard plants are perennial, growing back year after year and developing deeper root systems each season. You could try to pull one of these little trees out of the ground, but the stems would most likely break, leaving the roots to regenerate a new plant.

That is the type of faith we are to have! Jesus put the emphasis on how great our God is, not how great our faith is. With only a tiny bit of faith, like a mustard seed, we can move mountains, and nothing shall be impossible.

As Christians, we need to stop measuring our faith by the size of the problem. We need to start looking instead at how great our God is. We need to plant that seed of faith—no matter how small—into whatever mountain stands in our way and believe it will be moved, because Jesus said it would.

> We need to stop measuring our faith
> by the size of the problem.

When Peter tried to walk on water, he made it only a few steps because he took his eyes off Jesus and fear dragged him down.

When he began to sink, Jesus lifted him up out of the water and said, "You of little faith" (Matt. 14:31). Peter did have little faith because that is what it took to walk on water.

If he could do that with just a little faith, imagine what will happen when that faith increases!

Remember the Faith

In the closing chapter of the Book of Hebrews, the writer tells us, "Remember your leaders, who spoke the word of God to you. Consider the outcome of their way of life and imitate their faith" (Heb. 13:7, NIV). As I asked before, if our Lord fasted, why would we think that we should not fast? There is no record of Jesus ever healing anyone until He returned from the forty days of fasting that launched His earthly ministry. Jesus said we would do even greater works than He had done, because He was returning to the Father. If Jesus did not begin to minister before fasting, how can we?

Throughout the history of the Christian church, God has raised up men and women who were willing to dedicate their lives to Him and diligently seek Him through fasting and prayer. Long seasons of fasting are credited for launching such revivals as seen by Evan Roberts in Laos, who fasted and prayed for thirteen months for that country. Healing evangelists like John Alexander Dowie, John G. Lake, Maria Woodworth-Etter, Smith Wigglesworth, and Kathryn Kuhlman all understood the tremendous power of faith in operation throughout their ministries.

Not Getting Through?

There may be times when you are fasting and praying and standing in faith, yet you still do not sense that anything is happening. There's no "sprout" showing through the dirt. Remember the faith of those before you. David said, "I humbled myself with fasting; and my prayer would return to my own heart. I paced about as though he were my friend or brother; I bowed down heavily, as one who mourns for his mother" (Ps. 35:13–14).

> The Lord will reward your diligence.

Do not let the enemy drag you down with discouragement. Remember, God gives you the garment of praise for the spirit of heaviness. Sometimes you will not feel like praying when you are fasting, but pray anyway. You will be amazed how God will show up, and it will be like all of heaven has come down and glory has filled your soul.

In this same psalm, David had not yet received an answer to his prayer, yet he was able to wait in faith, proclaiming the praises of God: "'Let the LORD be magnified, who has pleasure in the prosperity of His servant.' And my tongue shall speak of Your righteousness and of Your praise all the day long" (vv. 27–28). The Lord will reward your diligence; His delight is in the prosperity—the wholeness—of His children.

Remember the faith of Abraham, "the substance of things hoped for, the evidence of things not seen" (Heb. 11:1). It was that faith that was accredited to him as righteousness—because he *believed* God. Even though Abraham's body was dead as far as fathering children was concerned, he still desired a child of his own. God desired it even more and gave him the promise of not only a son but also descendants more numerous than the stars of the sky (Gen. 15:4–6). When you believe God for something, you are exercising faith, which pleases Him. Are you dreaming the dreams of God for your life and your family? Are you believing Him for those *things*—those evidences—to come to pass?

Now He who searches the hearts knows what the mind of the Spirit is, because He makes intercession for the saints according to the will of God. And we know that all things work together for good to those who love God, to those who are the called according to His purpose.

—ROMANS 8:27–28

Chapter 13

God's Priorities

It seems unnecessary to begin this chapter by pointing out how God's priorities are seldom our priorities. That is the difference in the nature of man and the nature of God. He even said so: "As the heavens are higher than the earth, so are my ways higher than your ways and my thoughts than your thoughts" (Isa. 55:9, NIV). So, how do we position ourselves to hear from God? How do we free ourselves from our own desires in order to know His will? Well, I can tell you from firsthand experience that fasting causes you to take that sword of God's Word and separate what you "want" from what you "need."

> There is no higher authority than to know the
> heart of God for a situation you are facing.

Let us therefore be diligent to enter that rest, lest anyone fall according to the same example of disobedience. For the word of God is living and powerful, and sharper than any two-edged sword, piercing even to the division of soul and spirit, and of joints and marrow, and is a discerner of the thoughts and intents of the heart. And there is no creature hidden from His sight, but all things are naked and open to the eyes of Him to whom we must give account.

—Hebrews 4:11–13

There is that word *diligent* again. Fasting, praying, and feeding on the Word of God puts that sword in your hand and positions you to discern the difference between your thoughts and God's thoughts. There is no higher authority than to know the heart of God for a situation you are facing. His Word is final!

Get in Line

Imagine living just doors away from where Jesus lived much of His earthly ministry and never getting swept up into His message or miracles. Cornelius is such a man. He must have been a rather busy man because he completely missed the move of God. Luke tells his story in the Book of Acts. He begins, "There was a certain man in Caesarea called Cornelius, a centurion of what was called the Italian Regiment, a devout man and one who feared God with all his household, who gave alms generously to the people, and prayed to God always" (Acts 10:1–2).

So we know that this generous, probably kind-hearted Italian man had been around the Jewish faith enough to begin to believe in their God and to pray to Him, but as yet, the gospel of salvation through the blood of Jesus was a message that had only come to the Jews, not to the Gentiles. Still, Cornelius was diligent—and his diligence is why those of us who are not of Jewish descent are able to call upon the name of the Lord and be saved today.

The Bible tells us that around the ninth hour of the day, an angel appeared to Cornelius and told him to send for Peter in Joppa and listen to what Peter would tell him. So he faithfully sent his most trusted men to Joppa to bring Peter back with them. Now, stop here and think a moment. Here's a man who is not born again but is devoted to God. Was he just at his house watching a game on TV when this angel appeared to him? Not hardly.

When Peter arrived at his house, Cornelius said, "Four days ago I was fasting until this hour; and at the ninth hour I prayed in my house, and behold, a man stood before me in bright clothing, and said, 'Cornelius, your prayer has been heard, and your alms are remembered in the sight of God'" (Acts 10:30–31).

Cornelius was fasting and praying. He was diligently seeking God when that angel came to tell him that his diligence was about to be greatly rewarded. Peter preached the gospel to them, and "while Peter was still speaking these words, the Holy Spirit fell upon all those who heard the word. And those of the circumcision who believed were astonished, as many as came with Peter, because the gift of the Holy Spirit had been poured out on the Gentiles also. For they heard them speak with tongues and magnify God" (vv. 44–46).

Those of us who are not of Jewish descent can thank one man for being diligent to seek the Lord and bring the message of the cross to the Gentiles. Cornelius gave to the poor and prayed often, but he was a lost man. Fasting puts you in the mainstream of God's priorities.

God established priorities as early as the Book of Genesis. His principle of first things is stated clearly:

> And it shall be, when the LORD brings you into the land of the Canaanites, as He swore to you and your fathers, and gives it to you, that you shall set apart to the LORD all that open the womb, that is, every firstborn that comes from an animal which you have; the males shall be the LORD's.
>
> —Exodus 13:11–12

Fasting puts you in the mainstream of God's priorities.

This is an amazing text to me. Throughout Scripture, God makes it clear that the firsts—firstlings of flocks, firstfruits of harvest, firstborn males of families—all belong to Him. The Old Testament is full of types and shadows of things revealed in the New Testament, namely that Jesus is the firstborn Son. Two thousand years ago, that spotless Lamb redeemed those of us who were made unclean by sin when He offered His own blood on the altar in heaven.

Go Vertical

For ten years and two hundred thirty episodes, the TV sitcom *Friends* became a focal point for millions in this country. In 1994, the critics said this show about six young single friends living in New York City was not very entertaining, clever, or original. The final episode of that show had 52 million viewers. The critics who said it wouldn't make it didn't take into account the great vacuum for connection in American culture. People want and need to be connected in relationships.

That need to be connected is evidenced in the church by home groups and a greater emphasis on community. While that is good, if we're not careful, we can become too horizontally focused and not sufficiently vertically focused. Church right now, for the most part in the

Western world, particularly in America, is all about *me*: "I want my needs met. Bless me; teach me; help me." While those are legitimate needs and desires, we must keep in mind that the cross has two beams: one is horizontal, but the other is vertical.

Fasting turns your priorities more vertical and more in line with God's desires. It's what Jesus did when He cleared the temple. The priorities had become excessively horizontal.

> Then Jesus went into the temple of God and drove out all those who bought and sold in the temple, and overturned the tables of the money changers and the seats of those who sold doves. And He said to them, "It is written, 'My house shall be called a house of prayer,' but you have made it a 'den of thieves.'"
>
> —MATTHEW 21:12–13

That doesn't mean that when you fast, you don't have specific needs and desires of your own for which you are seeking God. Indeed, you should fast for a specific purpose. However, I believe that as you continue on a prolonged fast, the true cry of your heart becomes:

"More of You, God, and less of me." When you put Him first, all else is added.

The Order of Things

I want to show you several key aspects of life that we tend to get out of order. First, we often miss the significance of Paul's words: "Now may the God of peace Himself sanctify you completely; and may your whole spirit, soul, and body be preserved blameless at the coming of our Lord Jesus Christ" (1 Thess. 5:23). Notice that God's priority is concern for your spirit first, your soul second, and your body third. We get that totally backward, always focusing on our bodies first and our spirits last. We worry about things such as: "What will I wear?" "What will I eat?" "Where do I need Botox?" Jesus told us not to worry about such things, saying, "Is not life more than food and the body more than clothing?" (Matt. 6:25).

According to God's principle of "first things," what you put first will order the rest. When you put your spirit first, you serve the things of the Holy Spirit rather than the desires of the flesh. As a result, your mind, will, emotions, as well as your physical body and health will fall in line according to the Spirit's leading. "For if you live according to the flesh you will die; but if by the Spirit you put to death the deeds of the body, you will live" (Rom. 8:13).

Forgiveness

Another area that too frequently becomes out of order has to do with reconciliation and public worship. Notice what is to be "first" according to Jesus: "If you bring your gift to the altar, and there remember that your brother has something against you, leave your gift there before the altar, and go your way. First be reconciled to your brother, and then come and offer your gift" (Matt. 5:23). First be reconciled. God desires our public and corporate worship. However, those public acts of worship do not fix our private acts of strife, contention, and unforgiveness.

What you put first will order the rest.

I heard a story once about a local woman who moved back to Georgia to purchase the old homestead on which she grew up. Her mother and father had passed away, and the land had to be claimed. One of the first things she had to do was hire someone to come clean out the well that her father dug many years before. Over the years, a lot of stuff had accumulated in the well and made the water worthless. The crew got a good-sized pile out and showed the woman so they could get paid for the job. But she said, "Nope. There's more in there. Please keep digging." This went on for about three days. Finally, at the end of the third day, the woman looked at the latest pile of trash, toys, and miscellaneous objects that had found their home at the bottom of the well and said, "You're done." Puzzled, one of the men asked how she knew that was it. She answered, "Because when I was a little girl and Papa first dug that well, I took a teapot and threw it in the well. I figured the first thing that went into that well would be the last thing that came out."

Fasting allows the Holy Spirit to come in, and just like those well diggers, He can begin to dig up stuff that needs to come out of your spirit. You will have a hard time accepting the grace and forgiveness of the

Lord if you haven't gotten down to that "teapot" in your own heart. You have to get out that first offense you stored up years ago, and sometimes, you will have to dig for a long time. But when you do get down to that teapot, the river of living water can spring back up out of you and refresh others. That is God's priority.

Dirty Cups

What else does the Lord expect us to keep first? In the words of Jesus, "Woe to you, scribes and Pharisees, hypocrites! For you cleanse the outside of the cup and dish, but inside they are full of extortion and self-indulgence. Blind Pharisee, first cleanse the inside of the cup and dish, that the outside of them may be clean also" (Matt. 23:25–26). Jesus was teaching the people to obey the laws of God taught by the Pharisees, but He instructed the crowd not to do as the Pharisees did. They had gone overboard into legalism, and in their extremes, had gotten things out of order. For example, they cleaned a pretty cup on the outside, but the inside was still full of crud that they had not cleaned out. Whether you are talking about your life or your cup, first clean the inside, because that makes all the rest much more presentable. Fasting will cause you to get the crud out, cleaning the inside, which will then make the outside clean.

Something in Your Eye?

Another "first" is found in Matthew chapter 7:

> Judge not, that you be not judged. For with what judgment you judge, you will be judged; and with the measure you use, it will be measured back to you. And why do you look at the speck in your brother's eye, but do not consider the plank in your own eye? Or how can you say to your brother, "Let me remove the speck from your eye"; and look, a plank is in your own eye? Hypocrite! First remove the plank from your own eye, and then you will see clearly to remove the speck out of your brother's eye.
>
> —MATTHEW 7:1–5

Before you will be ready to perceive wrong in someone else's life, you first need to do a little self-examination of your own life. You're worried about a tiny splinter in their eye when you have a telephone pole in your own. Hypocrisy is judging somebody else when there is something worse going on in you. Our attitude and lifestyle should be as Paul directed the church in Galatia:

> Brethren, if a man is overtaken in any trespass, you who are spiritual restore such a one in a spirit of gentleness, considering yourself lest you also be tempted. Bear one another's burdens, and so fulfill the law of Christ. For if anyone thinks himself to be something, when he is nothing, he deceives himself.
>
> —GALATIANS 6:1–3

The word *restore* used here comes from a Greek medical term meaning to reset, like one would set a shoulder that's out of joint. Sometimes we need to remember that someone may be out of joint, but they are not out of the body of Christ. When saints get out of joint, they need tender hands. They need trained hands to reset and restore them.

Kingdom First

I've touched on this briefly, but this is another area that Christians tend to get out of order. Jesus said, "So do not worry, saying, 'What shall we eat?' or 'What shall we drink?' or 'What shall we wear?' For the pagans run after all these things, and your heavenly Father knows that you need them. But seek first his kingdom and his righteousness, and all these things will be given to you as well" (Matt. 6:31–33, NIV). Again, fasting helps you to distinguish between what you want and what you really need. When you choose not to worry about these things and to seek Him first, you are demonstrating the kind of faith that is pleasing to God, because you are trusting Him to also give you all the things you need.

If poverty has killed its thousands, prosperity has killed its tens of thousands. We all need to heed the warning of Jesus: "Take heed to yourselves, lest at any time your hearts be overcharged with surfeiting [overindulgence], and drunkenness, and cares of this life" (Luke 21:34, KJV).

First Love

What would your answer be if the Lord asked you, "Do you remember the last time you were lovesick for Me?" I began to ponder that question recently. I thought back to the time when Cherise and I were dating. We were deeply in love and wanted to spend every moment together. It was probably a good thing our parents wouldn't let us because we would have surely starved to death. For the longest time, whenever we would go out to eat, we would end up taking about three bites because we were so engrossed with each other. I know that sounds a little sappy, but stay with me—I have a point. I cannot tell you the money I wasted on meals, simply because our desire to talk and spend time with each other was greater than our desire for food. We were "lovesick" for each other. As I thought back on that, it hit me. That is what the Lord feels when we fast. When we are so lovesick for our first love, fasting is easy.

> Do you remember the last time you were lovesick for God?

So I ask you, do you remember the last time you walked away from a meal because you were so pre-occupied with your first love that the food was of no interest? Have you experienced seasons when it felt like the Bridegroom was distant? You just don't sense His presence as close as you once did. You have no heart for worship and you lack the excitement and childlike enthusiasm you once had for spiritual things. Perhaps it is time to stop the busyness of your everyday life and declare a fast, a season of lovesickness to restore the passion of your first love back to its proper place in your life. When you fast, everything slows down. The days seem longer. The nights seem longer, but in the quietness of seeking, you will find Him whom your heart desires.

Walk about Zion, and go all around her. Count her towers; mark well her bulwarks; consider her palaces; that you may tell it to the generation following. For this is God, our God forever and ever; He will be our guide even to death.

—Psalm 48:12–14

Chapter 14

For the Little Ones

There is another very important priority on God's agenda, and for this one, I needed an entire chapter. God sees far beyond what our limited minds can comprehend. For the most part, whenever we hear Joshua's words, "As for me and my house, we will serve the LORD" (Josh. 24:15), we think of our spouses, our children, maybe even our grandchildren. God sees generations.

In the more recent corporate fasts at Free Chapel, the Lord has laid on my heart this passage from Ezra:

> Then I proclaimed a fast there, at the river of Ahava, that we might afflict ourselves before our God, to seek of him a right way for us, and for our little ones, and for all our substance. For I was ashamed to require of the

king a band of soldiers and horsemen to help us against the enemy in the way: because we had spoken unto the king, saying, The hand of our God is upon all them for good that seek him; but his power and his wrath is against all them that forsake him. So we fasted and besought our God for this: and he was intreated of us.

—Ezra 8:21–23, kjv

> We fast because we need to know
> the right way for our lives.

After seventy years of Babylonian captivity, Ezra was about to lead the remnant of Israel—an entire generation of young people who had never seen the temple of Jerusalem, including some very small children—back to the Holy Land. It was going to be a treacherous journey home, but they had boasted of God's mighty hand of protection before heading out, so they had to act in faith and believe their own words. Settled by the river, Ezra proclaimed a fast so that the people might humble themselves before God and seek His face. They needed to know the way they should take, for their protection and for the protection of their little ones.

We fast because we need to know the right way for our lives. We do not need to be confused as to our future or the choices before us. Fast, seek His face, and have faith that He will guide you. Should you take that new job? Should you marry her? Should you marry him? It is biblical to fast and seek God for the right direction for your life. Examples are found in Judges 20:26 (Israel seeking to know if they should go into battle against the tribe of Benjamin), 1 Samuel 7:6 (seeking God at Mizpeh for forgiveness and protection against the Philistine army), and 2 Chronicles 20:3 (Jehoshaphat inquiring about the army that was about to attack).

We also fast for our little ones. I had not noticed the tenderness in that language before. Usually it is assumed that there were children in the midst of the pilgrims. But here, Ezra sees such promise, such potential, and such grave danger for the next generation. It was tempting to request an army to go with them. Perhaps Ezra remembered the old song of David:

> Now I know that the LORD saves his
> anointed;

> he answers him from his holy heaven
>> with the saving power of his right hand.
> Some trust in chariots and some in horses,
>> but we trust in the name of the LORD our
>> God.
> They are brought to their knees and fall,
>> but we rise up and stand firm.

—PSALM 20:6–8, NIV

A few verses later, we see that God heard and answered their prayers. Fasting with prayer just seems to open a different frequency in God's ear! Ezra recorded that they left the river Ahava after twelve days to set out for Jerusalem. He also testified, "The hand of our God was on us, and he protected us from enemies and bandits along the way" (Ezra 8:31, NIV). God's hand was upon them, His right hand protecting them and their little ones!

The Unblushables

Today, if we have lost anything in this country, we have lost the *right* way. Yet I ask you, who is fasting for the protection of our little ones in this age?

Today, fasting has all but disappeared from regular Christian discipline. We have more media availability for preaching than ever before, yet sin and repentance are seldom preached.

Today, our little ones are exposed to every kind of perversion and danger with a click of a button—be it TV, Internet, cell phones, or just a stroll through the local mall.

Today, the words of the weeping prophet Jeremiah cause a lump in my throat as I read them aloud. Speaking of a sinful generation, the Lord said:

> Are they ashamed of their loathsome conduct? No, they have no shame at all; they do not even know how to blush. So they will fall among the fallen; they will be brought down when I punish them.
>
> —JEREMIAH 6:15, NIV

Our only boast is in our God!

In an age where gay and lesbian experimentation is considered normal on campuses, when oral sex and every type of perversion imaginable is just winked at (kids call that "technical virginity" now), when sexual affairs before and after marriage are totally acceptable, our little ones are positioned to be an unblushable generation. Already they are becoming so familiar with sin that when they see immodest filth, they giggle when they should instead blush and turn away.

There is an enemy that is taking captive entire generations in America today. Its grip is getting tighter and tighter—reaching farther and farther. We are standing at the crossroads. "Stand at the crossroads and look; ask for the ancient paths, ask where the good way is, and walk in it, and you will find rest for your souls" (Jer. 6:16, NIV).

> We need to learn to trust the reliability
> of Scripture when things get crazy.

We have the opportunity to stand up like Ezra, to declare a holy fast for our children (Ezra 8:21), and to seek the Lord for the right way to lead this generation. Since we have been fasting at Free Chapel, we are already seeing God's hand leading us. My oldest daughter, Courteney, completed the full twenty-one-day fast this year. She is a junior in high school and has become very aware of her own salvation and of the times in which we live. I believe as a result of the fast, she came to me recently with urgency in her heart and said, "Daddy, I love God, but I still don't know what His plan is for me. I don't know who I am, and I don't know what God wants me to do."

We need to learn to trust the reliability of Scripture when things get crazy. God's promises are your "gauges" when the storm of life rages. A man in our church is a pilot, and he sometimes lets me fly with him. He has taught me a few things about flying. The most crucial thing is to train yourself to rely on what the gauges in the plane tell you. When you fly a small plane into a storm, that plane is bounced in every direction, and you cannot rely on what you feel. Your equilibrium gets out of balance, and you won't know if you're flying right side up. The only thing that will take you safely through is relying on the gauges—relying on the Scriptures.

It is humbling to shut your mind off to what worldly wisdom and insight says is right and yield your trust to a few digital gauges on an airplane dashboard, but there's a lesson in that. James said:

> Scripture says: "God opposes the proud but gives grace to the humble." Submit yourselves, then, to God. Resist the devil, and he will flee from you. Come near to God and he will come near to you. Wash your hands, you sinners, and purify your hearts, you double-minded. Grieve, mourn and wail. Change your laughter to mourning and your joy to gloom. Humble yourselves before the Lord, and he will lift you up.
>
> —JAMES 4:6–10, NIV

Daniel humbled himself before the Lord. He fasted and prayed for three weeks, and an angel came to him and said, "Do not be afraid, Daniel. Since the first day that you set your mind to gain understanding and to humble yourself before your God, your words were heard, and I have come in response to them" (Dan. 10:12, NIV).

I want you to understand that you are not "twisting God's arm" when you go on a fast. You are not going to make God do anything He does not want to do.

What you are actually doing is positioning yourself and preparing your heart for what is to come. If you are willing to seek Him, He will be willing to give.

Any time you fast, it is a hunger strike against hell. Fasting is an extreme in-your-face statement to the devil—that same deceiver who used food to tempt Adam and Eve to sin. Gandhi was a humble Indian leader who went up against the British Empire for the freedom of his nation. He didn't fight them with violence. He would simply go on a hunger strike, and the attention of the world was drawn to his plight.

When we fast, we are effectively going on a hunger strike against hell to say, "Loose those who are bound by deception, lies, alcohol, drugs, pornography, false religion, etc!"

> Anytime you fast, it is a hunger strike against hell.

One Sunday morning as I arrived at Free Chapel, a faithful woman from our congregation met me at the door. She had been fasting for twenty-one days and had a wonderful report. She began:

My husband and I made it a matter of prayer during the fast to focus on the unsaved people in our family. I have two nieces who are sixteen and fourteen, and a sixty-year-old brother—all are practicing Buddhists. My sixteen-year-old niece has accepted Jesus as her Savior, and about ten days into the fast, my fourteen-year-old niece got saved. Not only that, but I was talking to my brother yesterday, and he told me that he accepted Jesus as his Savior, which is a miracle!

Another lady shared this testimony with the congregation:

I guess about six weeks ago, I gave you my children's names and asked you to pray for them because none of them were saved. My oldest is twenty-six. The rest are twenty, eighteen, and thirteen. My twenty-six-year-old decided two weeks later that he was going to move to Texas and live with my sister and her husband because he had a job offer just out of the blue.

After you counseled with me about this, Pastor, I decided just to hand it over to the

Lord no matter what happened. After he got to Texas, he called me and said, "Mom, Aunt Angela (my sister) said that if I was to stay here with them and live with them that I was going to have get up and go to church with them every Sunday."

I turned the phone away and said, "Hallelujah!" I told him, "Then go, son." He said, "OK." Their church is a small, Bible-believing church. He started going with them and called me a week later. He asked, "Mom, are you coming down for Christmas?" I said, "Yes, I'm coming to see you."

He said, "Would you get me a Bible for Christmas?" And I said, "OK…what does that mean?" My son answered, "Mom, I've been saved!"

Something you need to know is that since my divorce, my oldest son has been a strong male figure in my home. All the other kids really look up to him, and with his salvation, they've been calling him about things and just confiding in him about things that they wouldn't tell me. So, I really feel like my other children are going to come to the Lord before this year is out.

A woman from San Antonio wrote to tell us:

My sister, my nephew, and I joined you and your church in the twenty-one-day fast this year for the first time. I am seeing the hand of God over me and my family. Things are changing, moving like never before. I saw my son sober and in his right mind for the first time in many years (he is thirty-five). God bless you and your church for being obedient to the Lord.

This next story was shared by a precious couple that is on staff with us at Free Chapel. The husband says:

While we were still dating, my wife's doctor told her that she would probably never bear children because of some issues that medication was not reversing. Her physician gave a low chance of things ever improving.

Shortly after getting married, we moved to Gainesville and were on staff with Free Chapel when we first heard the twenty-one-day fasting message by Pastor Franklin. His message encouraged everyone to believe for four rewards during the fast, one of which was a physical healing. Every morning, we would take Communion and pray the fasting focus. On the twenty-first and final day of the fast, there was a celebration service where we would all break our fast together. My wife had been feeling tired, and just for the sake of it, she took a pregnancy test. Sure enough, she was pregnant!

We joke that we weren't trying or even asking for signs and wonders, but God delivered a wonderful confirmation of our faith on the final day of our sacrifice to Him. Suddenly, there was this womb that doctors said would never exist. Our OB was a Christian, and he would joke with us during our monthly visits. Here was another by-the-book checkup: perfect measurements, perfect weight gain. What's more, my wife was never sick during her pregnancy and never had any complications. Caden became so comfortable that he was actually a week late.

After five pushes and a half hour of delivery, a healthy eight-pound-five-ounce baby boy was born. Caden has been in the 95 percentile for his weight and height since being born, and all of this from a five-feet-two-inch mother who only weighs one hundred five pounds dripping wet. Our son has yet to be sick, break a bone, or end up in the hospital for an earache. Caden was also born on my birthday, a pretty cool coincidence, and he will turn four this October.

It is time for parents to stand up like Ezra and fast, seeking God for His right way and for His protection over this generation. Our little ones are waiting.

For the word of God is living and powerful, and sharper than any two-edged sword, piercing even to the division of soul and spirit, and of joints and marrow, and is a discerner of the thoughts and intents of the heart.

—Hebrews 4:12

Chapter 15

Is Your Blade Sharp Enough?

Can you imagine having an extended conversation with not just any angel, but one of the higher-ranking angels of God? Suppose that angel came to you and told you of kingdoms that would rise and fall in coming years, even explaining what principalities would manipulate those leaders and how alliances would form and be crushed as new kings rose to power. I'd be willing to give up a Twinkie or a T-bone steak for a few weeks in order to have my spirit open enough to receive such a visitation!

Of course, I'm talking about Daniel, the faithful man of God who was held captive in Babylon for most of his life. After Nebuchadnezzar besieged Jerusalem and took captives back to Babylon, he had the best and brightest of the young men set apart. They were to be trained for three years in the ways of the Chaldeans to eventually become his personal assistants. Daniel was among those selected, along with his three friends whom we have come to know by their Babylonian names: Shadrach, Meshach, and Abed-nego. Early on, Daniel and his friends set themselves apart from the others by refusing to defile themselves with the foods laid out for them on the king's table.

Notice that by simply taking such a stand, "God granted Daniel favor and compassion in the sight of the commander of the officials" (Dan. 1:9, NASU). Daniel explained that he and his friends would be in better shape after ten days of eating only vegetables and drinking only water than the others would be after eating the king's delicacies. The overseer continued giving them only their requested vegetables and water: "God gave them knowledge and intelligence in every branch of literature and wisdom; Daniel even understood all kinds of visions and dreams" (Dan. 1:17, NASU).

> It is time we set ourselves apart to seek the Lord and find understanding.

Daniel rose to positions of great responsibility within the kingdom of Babylon, even under subsequent rulers. In chapter 10, Daniel, then close to ninety years old, received a message of great conflict and a vision, both of which he understood. Apparently troubled, he recorded, "In those days I, Daniel, was mourning three full weeks. I ate no pleasant food, no meat or wine came into my mouth" (Dan. 10:2–3). The Hebrew word used here for "pleasant food" is *lechem*, or breads. So for twenty-one days, Daniel fasted all sweets, breads, and meats, and drank only water.

It was soon after that fast when Daniel's encounter with the angel of God took place along the Tigris River. Notice something very encouraging in what the angel told Daniel: his prayers had been heard in heaven from the very first day he started the fast (Dan. 10:12)! The only reason the angel had not appeared to Daniel sooner was because he was fighting with the principality of Persia (modern-day Iran).

Dull but Comfortable

Of the many different types of fasts that are acceptable, what has come to be called the Daniel fast is probably one of the more common—and with good reason. It is one of the personal fasts recorded in the Bible that brought with it great favor from the Lord. For twenty-one days, you eat only vegetables and fruits and drink only water. No colas, burgers, Twinkies, meats, sweets, or bread.

In the times in which we now live—when the enemy is taking our youth captive to sin at an alarming rate, when acts of Iraqi terrorism claim hundreds of lives, and when perversion is at an all-time high—like Daniel, it is time we set ourselves apart to seek the Lord and find understanding. Paul said:

> Finally, be strong in the Lord and in his mighty power. Put on the full armor of God so that you can take your stand against the devil's schemes. For our struggle is not against flesh and blood, but against the rulers, against the authorities, against the powers of this dark world and against the spiritual forces of evil in the heavenly realms. Therefore put on the full armor of God, so that when the day of evil comes, you may be able to stand your ground, and after you have done everything, to stand. Stand firm

> then, with the belt of truth buckled around your waist, with the breastplate of righteousness in place, and with your feet fitted with the readiness that comes from the gospel of peace. In addition to all this, take up the shield of faith, with which you can extinguish all the flaming arrows of the evil one. Take the helmet of salvation and the sword of the Spirit, which is the word of God.
>
> —EPHESIANS 6:10–17, NIV

Have you ever seen a military man try to fit into his uniform thirty years later? Usually, it won't even come close to buttoning down the front. When you're a soldier, you stay fit; you stay healthy, alert, and ready. Paul said we should live that way because the days are evil. The enemy prowls around waiting to attack. Just as the angel told Daniel, principalities of nations rise up to do battle, but we live as retired military, growing fat and comfortable.

Moses fasted. Elijah fasted forty days. Paul fasted fourteen days. Jesus fasted forty days. If the children of God do not fast, how will we ever fit into the armor of God? How will we effectively wield the sword of the Spirit?

I want you to understand something: fasting and prayer sharpen the blade, which is the Word of God. When you fast, mealtimes often become study times. You become more keyed in to God's Word, and God begins to show you deeper truths. It wasn't after finishing off a bag of chocolate-covered doughnuts that Daniel got the visit from the angel. Daniel began to understand God's truths after fasting and getting alone with Him. Understanding comes from the study of God's Word!

Many Christians have just stopped fighting all together because they are battered and bruised or using dull blades to fight demonic powers. When you fast and pray, you effectively sharpen the Word in your mouth. Instead of flippantly quoting Scripture, you now wield a powerful weapon with a razor-sharp edge that slashes the enemy when you speak.

> When you fast and pray, you sharpen
> the Word of God in your mouth.

Amazing, isn't it? Simply by missing some meals and setting your heart on understanding by studying

God's Word, you please God, you release beauty for ashes and joy for mourning, and the garment of praise defeats the spirit of heaviness. Your praise goes forth and scatters the enemy, you develop patience, you come in line with God's priorities, you loose angelic messengers, and you find God's right way for you and protection for your little ones. When are we going to take dominion back from King Stomach and seek diligently after the kingdom of God in this way?

America Like Nineveh

America has greatly sinned against God through abortion, homosexuality, adultery, rampant pornography, and fornication. We have no fear of God, and America is rapidly becoming a pagan nation. Our only hope is to humble ourselves in fasting and prayer.

Nineveh was a great city. In fact, the Bible states that it was so vast it took three days just to tour it. Historians say Nineveh had walls 100 feet high with watchtowers that stretched another 100 feet. The walls were so thick that chariots could race on top of them. Surrounding the city of about 120,000 people was a vast moat 150 feet wide and 60 feet deep. Nineveh was proud, strong, and impregnable. And if any foreign army wanted to lay siege or attempted to surround and cut them off, they had enough supplies to hold out for at least twenty years. But Nineveh was filled with sin.

I want to stop there a moment and point something out. I'm sure not all the people of Nineveh were sinning. There were children and probably plenty of common, decent, God-fearing people, but remember what happened in the battle of Ai? Joshua and the people of Israel had just defeated Jericho. Yet one man took the holy things that were devoted to God and hid them amongst his own belongings. When Joshua sought the Lord after that crushing blow from such a tiny city, God said, "Israel has sinned" (Josh. 7:11). Only one man took the devoted things, but he brought sin on the entire camp. He was stoned along with his wife and children.

Daniel's fast and visitation from the angel is recorded in Daniel 10. Throughout chapter 9, Daniel cries out to the Lord on behalf of all Israel, saying over and over, "We have sinned and done wrong. We have been wicked and rebelled....we have sinned against you" (vv. 5, 11). Daniel identified with the sin of his nation, though we see no sin that Daniel himself had committed.

God sent Jonah to preach repentance to Nineveh. He proclaimed, "Forty more days and Nineveh will be overturned" (Jon. 3:4, NIV). It is very possible that the people of Nineveh had some understanding of how powerful the God of Israel was, because they were struck with fear at these words and believed them. They declared a fast, and the king even issued a decree that no man or animal was to taste food or even water. Without any guarantee, he thought by humbling themselves in this manner, God may "relent and with compassion turn from his fierce anger so that we will not perish" (v. 9, NIV).

God did turn from His anger and spare the city, but they again ceased to seek the Lord. About a hundred years later, the prophet Nahum prophesied judgment on that city: "The LORD has given a command concerning you, [Nineveh]: 'You will have no descendants to bear your name. I will destroy the carved images and cast idols that are in the temple of your gods. I will prepare your grave, for you are vile'" (Nah. 1:14, NIV).

America has had its times and seasons. America is a faith-filled, God-fearing nation—pledging allegiance to our country with the words, "One nation, under God, indivisible..." We chose to imprint our coins and money with the words "In God We Trust," in order to set ourselves apart as a nation that honored God with our finances and our lives. Many a fiery evangelist has brought the message of repentance to our nation: Charles Finney, Dwight L. Moody, Jonathan Edwards, John Wesley, Billy Sunday, William Booth, and, of course, Billy Graham, just to name a few. Many waves of revival have swept our country. God is merciful to send many Jonahs to give us the opportunity to fast, pray, and repent, but how long will He wait? When will a Nahum rise up and prophesy the swift judgment of an angry God on America?

He heard Daniel on the very first day!

We are living in important days and in important times. This book contains multiple testimonies of people who have received tremendous personal reward and blessing over just a few years because they teamed up with one church, one ministry here in America that corporately fasts and prays. Thankfully, churches across this country are coming to understand the importance of fasting and humbling ourselves before God.

We can humble ourselves and pray and seek His face and expect Him to hear from heaven and heal our land (2 Chron. 7:14). He heard Daniel on the very first day!

Yom Kippur

Yom Kippur is perhaps the most celebrated holy day on the Jewish calendar. Meaning "Day of Atonement," it was established by God for Israel:

> This shall be a statute forever for you: In the seventh month, on the tenth day of the month, you shall afflict your souls, and do no work at all, whether a native of your own country or a stranger who dwells among you. For on that day the priest shall make atonement for you, to cleanse you, that you may be clean from all your sins before the LORD.
>
> —LEVITICUS 16:29–30

Notice again the word *afflict*, which means fasting. Even Jews who typically do not observe any other

Jewish festival will often participate in Yom Kippur by fasting, attending synagogue, and refraining from work to atone for sins against God. Yom Kippur, or the Day of Atonement, is the final day of "appeal" to God for atonement, which is preceded by ten Days of Awe that are spent in reflection on one's life and sins.

It was on Yom Kippur in 1963 that the nations of Egypt, Jordan, and Syria allied to attack Israel and wipe out that nation. All of Israel had been fasting and repenting of sin before God for twenty-four hours. The allied enemies of Israel picked the wrong day to attack.

History records that the soldiers literally ran out of the synagogues to the front lines, having had nothing to eat for twenty-four hours. At first, the battle was going toward the Arab armies who pushed Israel back for three days. It appeared that victory for Israel was impossible, but the battle turned on the third day. Even though they were significantly outnumbered, Israel's army was victorious and took back what ground they lost, plus even more. Today, when you hear news reports about things happening in the "occupied territories," remember that those are the additional lands Israel claimed in the Yom Kippur War. The enemy thinks you are weaker when you fast. He will try to convince you that you are dying without food—but you are not. God is preparing to breathe life into your situation to open a door to His promises.

Continual Prayer

Fasting is not a means to promote yourself. The greatest thing fasting will do for you will be to break down all of the stuff that accumulates from this world that blocks you from clear communion with the Father.

As the first section of this book mentions, when you are on a prolonged fast, you are praying continually. You have to make time to get away and pray, whether you feel like it or not. Fasting in and of itself is a continual prayer to God. You are praying twenty-four hours a day when you are fasting. If you have been fasting all day, you've been praying all day.

Some of the greatest miracles, breakthroughs, and seasons of prayer I have ever experienced did not come when I was "feeling led" to pray and fast. They actually came when the last thing I wanted to do was drag myself to my prayer place, but I did, and God honored my faithfulness. Jesus said, "When you pray...when you fast...when you give..." (Matt. 6). He expects those who follow Him to do these things whether feeling a special *leading* or not. These things should be part of every believer's life.

There are different levels of fasts. When I first started, I didn't start with twenty-one days. I just did three days, and then I built up to seven days, and then to twenty-one days. What I have done recently is a total fast for seven days in January and then a total fast for three days each month from February to December. That is a total of forty days over the course of a year.

Keep your armor fit and your blade sharp!

As you fast, target your unsaved loved ones in prayer. Create a "hit list" of people you want to see saved. It is good to be very specific in your prayers during a fast. What is the one most critical thing you want God to do in your life? God told Habakkuk to "write the vision and make it plain" (Hab. 2:2). I dare you to write down the names of those you want to see saved, and when you fast and pray, call those names out to God. As we have seen evidenced here at Free Chapel, I believe you too will see breakthroughs like you never dreamed!

If you let it, your flesh will take over and rule your life. That is why times of fasting are so crucial to your walk with God. Fasting helps you establish dominion and authority over your flesh. "Do not be deceived, God is not mocked; for whatever a man sows, that he will also reap. For he who sows to his flesh will of the flesh reap corruption, but he who sows to the Spirit will of the Spirit reap everlasting life. And let us not grow weary while doing good, for in due season we shall reap if we do not lose heart" (Gal. 6:7–9). Keep your armor fit and your blade sharp!

If My people who are called by My name will humble themselves, and pray and seek My face, and turn from their wicked ways, then I will hear from heaven, and will forgive their sin and heal their land. Now My eyes will be open and My ears attentive to prayer made in this place.

—2 Chronicles 7:14–15

Chapter 16

Seen but Not Heard

Is it possible to fast and the Lord not hear your plea? God said of Israel, "You cannot fast as you do today and expect your voice to be heard on high" (Isa. 58:4, NIV). What were they doing wrong?

Israel was unrepentant and had forsaken the ordinances of God. Though they appeared to be seeking God and delighting in His ways, their sin was all God could see. Instead of truly humbling themselves before God, fasting had become just another faithless mechanical performance full of strife, anger, and lashing out.

Though you do not fast to be cleansed of sin (the blood of Jesus is the only solution for sin), you should enter a fast seriously, having repented of any known sins. Fasting will even bring hidden things to the surface so you can repent. As David said, "Who may ascend into the hill of the LORD? Or who may stand in His holy place? He who has clean hands and a pure heart, who has not lifted up his soul to an idol, nor sworn deceitfully" (Ps. 24:3–4, NIV).

> You should enter a fast seriously, having repented of any known sins.

When you fast, your appearance should be normal, and you should not draw attention to your "affliction" of fasting through your actions, your treatment of others, or your temperament. Though your focus should be on your own needs, the needs of others should be on your heart as well. God said:

> Is this not the fast that I have chosen: to loose the bonds of wickedness, to undo the heavy burdens, to let the oppressed go free, and that you break every yoke? Is it not to share your bread with the hungry, and that you bring to your house the poor who are cast out; when you see the naked, that you cover him, and not hide yourself from your own flesh?
>
> —ISAIAH 58:6–7

The Israelites questioned why they fasted with no answer from God. The Lord called Isaiah to "cry aloud, spare not" (Isa. 58:1), telling the people to repent of their transgressions, to fast the way God ordained, and to tell them what would happen when they do:

> Then your light shall break forth like the morning, your healing shall spring forth speedily, and your righteousness shall go before you; the glory of the LORD shall be your rear guard. Then you shall call, and the LORD will answer; you shall cry, and He will say, "Here I am."
>
> —ISAIAH 58:8–9

Shining Light

What does "your light shall break forth like the morning" mean? Illumination. Jesus said, "You are the light of the world. A city that is set on a hill cannot be hidden" (Matt. 5:14). God intended Israel to be a "light" in darkness to other nations, glorifying the God of creation by their actions and by the blessings of God apparent on their lives, thus drawing others to God. Likewise, in our lives as children of God, our light will break forth and be apparent to others—I imagine much like the glow on the face of Moses when he descended the mountain after spending time with God. I really believe that God has brought illumination to my life and to my ministry, for which I can take no credit. Our TV ministry is reaching further than ever. A viewer wrote recently that she had gone on a forty-day fast from meat. She said:

> I had never completed a fast of this length, but using the book really helped me to remain steadfast. I heard God clearer than I've ever heard Him, and my life will never be the same. Thank you for the opportunity to partner with you and your ministry. God is truly using you in a powerful way to minister to His people and to the lost.

Health Springs Forth

I have to let these testimonies explain this point. My friend, Bob Rodgers, is a pastor in Kentucky. He has been on sixteen twenty-one-day fasts and six forty-day fasts. This testimony is about a man in his church who had lost his bridgework (teeth) and couldn't find them anywhere, so he had a new bridge made and joined in the first of the year fast.

Somewhere around the fourteenth day of their fast, the man began to cough pretty severely. In fact, he got into such a coughing fit that he coughed up something solid—his original bridgework! This is a true story! Apparently they had come loose in the night, and he had somehow aspirated them into his lung. (He must be a *really* deep sleeper!) It's one thing to be sick and be healed speedily. It is another for God to heal you of an issue before it makes you sick. Had that foreign object stayed in his lung much longer, he would have become very ill and required major surgery to have it removed.

A woman e-mailed this awesome testimony. She had been plagued for a few years with protruding "knots" at the base of her spine. You could place your hand on her back and feel them very easily. They caused her severe, sometimes debilitating pain. She and her husband were part of our twenty-one-day fast at the beginning of the year. The first three days they went on a total fast, drinking only water, and then a Daniel fast for the remaining eighteen days. On the second day, her back was hurting badly with no relief. She went over her prayer list, calling out the names of unsaved family members and other needs and asking the Lord to please heal her back. On the third day, she was praying over her list and asking the Lord again to heal the knots. She placed her hand on them to lay hands on herself, only to find that they were no longer there! She had been completely healed on just the second day of her fast and had not even realized it!

This letter also attests to health springing forth speedily from fasting:

> Our son is nineteen years old and was diagnosed with cystic fibrosis at the age of five. Recently, he was admitted to the hospital because his oxygen level had fallen to 70 percent. About a week after the fast ended, he turned critical, and I was notified that his lungs could fail at any moment. I immediately called my husband, spiritual friends, and family. I called a solemn assembly of prayer and fasting for twenty-four hours, beginning at 5:00 p.m. that Thursday until 5:00 p.m. Friday. Needless to say at 4:00 p.m.

Friday, the twenty-third hour of the fast, my
son's carbon dioxide test came back normal.
There was nothing the medical doctor could
do. God is faithful. I'm so thankful for my
church at Free Chapel and their obedience to
obey God in prayer and fasting. My husband,
my twenty-one-year-old son, and I have been
involved in this twenty-one-day fast and are
thankful it was going on during this time.

Righteousness

The Lord says that when you fast, "your righteousness
shall go before you" (Isa. 58:8).

Your faith, your right standing with God, will
cause you to move into areas where you would not
have moved if you had not fasted. Doors will open
to you that were not opened before, and your influence will go out like ripples in a pond. One woman
wrote: "I joined two friends in a twenty-one-day fast,
after which the Holy Spirit delivered to me a special
message about fasting. At His prodding I typed out
the message and have shared it with others. Praise the
Lord—the message touched hearts and helped others

to understand the power of fasting. It is exciting to hear what God is doing in their lives because of their faithfulness to fast."

As I said before, when my brother and I started our first revival meetings, we took turns fasting. I would fast on the days he preached, and he would fast the days I preached. We knew we had the right intentions in mind, but we were a little surprised when that two- or three-day revival lasted several weeks. We looked like half-starved refugees when the revival ended, but we had tapped into something powerful. I believe the doors that have been opened to me have been a direct result of His promises being fulfilled because of fasting. There are people whose lives can be forever made better because of your righteousness going forth with influence.

Rearguard

Most of us have heard the slang expression: "I've got your back." It means that someone you trust is watching out for anything that may try to sneak up behind you and bring you harm. When you fast, Isaiah said, "The God of Israel will be your rear guard" (Isa. 52:12).

> From the first day that Daniel began to fast, God heard.

Further, God says, "No weapon formed against you shall prosper, and every tongue which rises against you in judgment you shall condemn. This is the heritage of the servants of the LORD, and their righteousness is from Me" (Isa. 54:17). No wonder the devil wants fasting to remain the best-kept secret in the kingdom.

He Will Hear and Answer

The Israelites were fasting, but with wrong motives. Without the right motives, they could not find God. But when we fast according to His plan, He says, "Then you shall call, and the LORD will answer; you shall cry, and He will say, 'Here I am'" (Isa. 58:9). Remember what the angel told Daniel in Daniel 10? From the first day that Daniel began to fast, God heard. The only thing that held up his answer was battle in the heavens!

A woman who volunteers for Free Chapel gave the most amazing testimony to this fact. Her parents had been in severe financial trouble for over a year. They had been given notice of foreclosure proceedings if they did not pay $5,500. She called her unsaved brothers and asked them if they wanted to join her in doing something that would help her parents in this desperate situation. God backed her up! Her brothers agreed, and they began to fast. Within fifteen days of the house being foreclosed, her parents received a phone call. Her father had applied for disability in 2000, but it took six years for them to get around to having the hearing on his case. They called to inform the family that his disability application had been approved, and a check was in the mail that very day in the amount of—are you ready for this?—$86,000, which included the retroactive amount from 2000. In addition, he would be getting disability payments monthly. There is no way her brothers can deny that God is the One who brought about this miracle.

God's promises don't stop there. He also says:

> Then shall thy light rise in obscurity, and thy darkness be as the noonday: and the LORD

shall guide thee continually, and satisfy thy soul in drought, and make fat thy bones: and thou shalt be like a watered garden, and like a spring of water, whose waters fail not. And they that shall be of thee shall build the old waste places: thou shalt raise up the foundations of many generations.

—ISAIAH 58:10–12, KJV

Obscurity and Darkness

Your light will rise out of obscurity. In other words, in situations you face that are just overwhelming and you don't know how to find your way through the darkness of obscurity and confusion, God will cause your light to shine on the path you are to take.

My friend, Pastor Bob Rodgers, had another wonderful testimony come forth out of his congregation. They go on a corporate fast each year just as we do here at Free Chapel. There was a man who lost his bakery business. Hard times hit, and the business went under just before the Christmas season. All he could afford to give his wife that year for Christmas was a seventy-five-cent card. In January, he joined the twenty-one-day fast.

At the end of the fast, he had an appointment to see his accountant in order to prepare his taxes and review the losses of the previous year. Now remember—he had fasted and sought God. When he arrived at the office, his accountant said, "I've been trying to call you, but your number has been disconnected. I heard about a man in Louisville who owns four bakeries. He wants to sell the businesses, and I thought about you. He wants to sell them for just twenty-five thousand dollars."

The man just kind of smirked and said, "I can't even afford to pay a twenty-five-dollar light bill right now. How can I come up with that kind of cash?" Still discouraged, the man left. On the way home he stopped at a stop sign. The white letters on the red background seemed more vivid than usual. While he was stopped, he sensed the Holy Spirit saying, "For twenty-one days you have asked Me to bless you, have you not? Turn back."

He immediately turned his car around and went back to ask for the name and number of the man selling the bakeries. Three men from his church gave him the money up front, and he was able to pay them back in full within six months. He could barely afford a card for his wife the Christmas before. At the end of their first year of giving their first days of the year to the Lord in fasting and prayer, he and his wife were so prosperous that she gave him an airplane for Christmas that year!

> You will raise up a foundation
> for many generations.

The Lord guided him back to His promise. That is another benefit of fasting: the Lord will guide you continually. Though the path before you may be obscure, when you fast and pray in faith, God will reward you and guide you. "Your ears shall hear a word behind you, saying, 'This is the way, walk in it'" (Isa. 30:21).

Raise a Foundation

Finally—and this is very close to my heart—when you fast, "you shall raise up the foundations of many generations" (Isa. 58:12). When you fast, you begin to lay a spiritual foundation that not only affects your life, but God says you will also affect the generations to come after you. I don't just fast for myself; I fast for my children, my future grandchildren, and so on. I have laid a foundation through my devotion to God that He will build upon because He found an inroad to my family. A woman who watches the *Kingdom Connection* broadcast on TBN wrote to share a remarkable testimony to this effect:

> I did my first twenty-one-day fast after seeing Pastor Franklin's teaching. I believe the Lord told me I would be fasting for my sick father, who was not yet a believer. I felt I had a promise from God that my dad would not leave this earth without my knowing he is saved. Nearly three months after the fast, my dad died. But as the Lord promised, three days before his death, he assured me that he had asked Jesus into his heart!
>
> I also fasted for my twenty-two-year-old prodigal daughter, who walked away from the Lord when she was eighteen. I began this year with the twenty-one-day Daniel fast, again with my daughter as my focus. I recently

heard from my daughter. She wanted to tell me that she is coming to church on Easter Sunday! It will be the first time in four and a half years. The Lord confirmed that this has occurred as a result of my fast. I am making fasting a discipline in my life.

Fasting can end the demonic attack on your family. Fasting can break the generational curses. When you fast, you lay a new foundation of blessing that will be transferred over to your children and your children's children. For this reason alone, I believe the head of any family who has ever been touched by divorce, abuse, molestation, etc. should designate a fast for your family and children in order to bind those demonic attachments from your generations. "And you shall be called the Repairer of the Breach, the Restorer of Streets to Dwell In" (Isa. 58:12).

Therefore, brethren, be even more diligent to make your call and election sure, for if you do these things you will never stumble; for so an entrance will be supplied to you abundantly into the everlasting kingdom of our Lord and Savior Jesus Christ.

—2 PETER 1:10–11

Chapter 17

Go for It

When the Israelites left Egypt, God provided manna for them daily, as well as clothing and shoes that did not wear out. Idolatry and unfaithfulness entered the hearts of the older generation, and they were left to wander in the wilderness for forty years. There was an entire generation that had grown up in the wilderness, listening to stories of the wonders that God had done to deliver Israel from Egyptian slavery—the plagues, the miracles, the plundering, the parting of the Red Sea, the drowning of Pharaoh's army, the fire by night and cloud by day, and the Ten Commandments written in stone. For nearly forty years, they ate manna in the morning and manna in the evening while wondering about a land flowing with milk and honey (Josh. 5:6).

Moses had been laid to rest. Joshua was now in charge, and things were changing. The command came from Joshua: "Sanctify yourselves, for tomorrow the LORD will do wonders among you" (Josh. 3:5). There must have been an extreme excitement spreading throughout the camp, but the Lord would do wonders only if the children of Israel would sanctify themselves.

The Hebrew root for *sanctify* is *qadhash*, which is also the root for *holy*. God said, "I am the LORD your God; consecrate yourselves and be holy, because I am holy" (Lev. 11:44, NIV). Sanctification is the process of becoming holy in daily life; it is practicing purity and being set apart from the world and from sin. Sanctification is allowing the Holy Spirit to make us more like Jesus in what we do, in what we think, and in what we desire. We do not hear much about sanctification from the pulpits these days, but if we are to see God do wonders in our midst, we must confront sin in our lives and live holy.

> **Fasting is an excellent means of sanctifying yourself.**

God was about to lead His chosen people out against the enemies of God, but they could not stand if they were not holy. This is clearly seen in the contrast between Israel's supernatural victory against the city of Jericho in Joshua 6 and their defeat in Joshua 7 by the tiny army of Ai after Israel had sinned by having stolen things in their midst.

Knowing God's Will

We desire to be in the will of God and to walk according to His plans. Sanctification is the key to being in God's will. As Paul said, "For this is the will of God, your sanctification" (1 Thess. 4:3). There is no need to try to find some mysterious "wheel of God" out there. You cannot follow God's leading until you start where Paul said start.

> It is God's will that you should be sanctified: that you should avoid sexual immorality; that each of you should learn to control his own body in a way that is holy and honorable, not in passionate lust like the heathen, who do not know God; and that in this matter no one

should wrong his brother or take advantage of him. The Lord will punish men for all such sins, as we have already told you and warned you. For God did not call us to be impure, but to live a holy life. Therefore, he who rejects this instruction does not reject man but God, who gives you his Holy Spirit.

—1 THESSALONIANS 4:3–8, NIV

> Fasting will help you identify areas of hidden sin in your life.

Fasting is an essential means of sanctifying yourself, pulling yourself away from the world, and getting closer to God. Fasting allows you to filter your life and to set yourself apart to seek the Lord. Jesus prayed for us:

They are not of the world, just as I am not of the world. Sanctify them by Your truth. Your word is truth. As You sent Me into the world, I also have sent them into the world. And for their sakes I sanctify Myself, that they also may be sanctified by the truth.

—JOHN 17:16–19

As I've stated in previous chapters, fasting will help you identify areas of even hidden sin and things that are displeasing to God in your life. Fasting helps you discern between serving the flesh and serving the spirit. "For if the blood of bulls and goats and the ashes of a heifer, sprinkling the unclean, sanctifies for the purifying of the flesh, how much more shall the blood of Christ, who through the eternal Spirit offered Himself without spot to God, cleanse your conscience from dead works to serve the living God?" (Heb. 9:13–14). If we are in Christ, His blood cleanses us from dead works, enabling us to serve God in holiness.

Necessity of Sanctification

Why do we need to sanctify ourselves? We have no place in our hearts for pride. We have no place in our hearts for complacency. If God has blessed your life, you are critically in need of sanctifying yourself. Beware of being a member of the "first church of the frozen chosen." Do not let the blessings of the past interfere with the blessings of the future. The blessings of the future will be greater than anything He has done in the past.

David was a man after God's heart, yet he cried out, "Create in me a clean heart, O God, and renew a steadfast spirit within me" (Ps. 51:10). We need a sanctification of *motives*. We need a sanctification of *desires*. We need a sanctification of *attitudes*. We need a sanctification of the *right spirit*. We need a sanctification of our *flesh*.

Responsibility of Sanctification

The writer of the Book of Hebrews warns, "Beware, brethren, lest there be in any of you an evil heart of unbelief in departing from the living God; but exhort one another daily, while it is called 'Today,' lest any of you be hardened through the deceitfulness of sin" (Heb. 3:12–13). While the leadership should certainly set an example in personal sanctification and holy living, it is the responsibility of every believer to "exhort" fellow believers. *Exhort* means to be abrasive with one another, to encourage one another, to push one another to live holy so that no one falls into temptation and ends up turning away from God.

Crossing Over

Joshua gave orders for the officers to command the children of Israel, saying:

> When you see the ark of the covenant of the LORD your God, and the priests, the Levites, bearing it, then you shall set out from your place and go after it. Yet there shall be a space between you and it, about two thousand cubits by measure. Do not come near it, that you may know the way by which you must go, for you have not passed this way before.
>
> —JOSHUA 3:3–4

They were to stand back and watch God. They were about to see the wonders they had heard about but never seen for themselves. As soon as the soles of their feet touched the water of the overflowing Jordan River, the waters separated as they had in the Red Sea, allowing the new generation to pass through the waters on dry ground. "Then the priests who bore the ark of the covenant of the LORD stood firm on dry ground in the midst of the Jordan; and all Israel crossed over on dry ground, until all the people had crossed completely over the Jordan" (v. 17).

When you fast and sanctify yourself unto God, it moves you off the bank and into the miracles! There are too many people on the edge of what God is doing and not enough of us standing firmly in the middle of His will. Do you want things to change in your home? You are the priest of your home—fast, sanctify yourself, and take a firm stand in the middle of God's will! When your family sees you stepping off the edge of mere "Sunday-morning religion" and getting right into the middle of what God is doing, they will follow and find God's direction for their lives.

> When you sanctify yourself unto God, it moves you off the bank and into the miracles!

I want you to notice that the children of Israel all crossed at the same place. You should be attached to a local body of believers instead of just trying to find your own way. If ever there was a time when we needed to be crossing together, taking a firm, united stand against sin in this nation, it is now. We need each other. We need a spirit of togetherness. We need a spirit of trust. We need a spirit of unity. We need a spirit of compassion for one another.

Blessing of Sanctification

Joshua's words went out to "the chosen generation." God had waited until all those who were stiff-necked and rebellious had grown old and died. That younger generation would go forth and inherit the promises. After they crossed the Jordan, God told Joshua to "make flint knives for yourself, and circumcise the sons of Israel again the second time" (Josh. 5:2). The older generation was circumcised, but the younger generation had not been. They were to bear the mark of covenant in their flesh before God would take them any further.

Circumcision speaks of sanctification of the flesh. It is cutting away dead things and hidden sins. You can look good publicly, raising your hands, giving your offerings, praying, and even fasting, but all the while hiding deadly sins. You are sanctified by the blood of Jesus when you first accept Him as your Lord and

Savior, but over time, complacency and hidden sins can creep into your heart. You can just start drifting, and you let your standard down. Paul explained this clearly to the Galatians:

> Now the works of the flesh are evident, which are: adultery, fornication, uncleanness, lewdness, idolatry, sorcery, hatred, contentions, jealousies, outbursts of wrath, selfish ambitions, dissensions, heresies, envy, murders, drunkenness, revelries, and the like; of which I tell you beforehand, just as I also told you in time past, that those who practice such things will not inherit the kingdom of God.
> —GALATIANS 5:19–21

The blessing of sanctification brings with it the promises of God's covenant and life in the Spirit: "The fruit of the Spirit is love, joy, peace, longsuffering, kindness, goodness, faithfulness, gentleness, self-control. Against such there is no law. And those who are Christ's have crucified the flesh with its passions and desires. If we live in the Spirit, let us also walk in the Spirit. Let us not become conceited, provoking one another, envying one another" (Gal. 5:22–26).

Fasting sharpens the blade and sharpens the Word in your heart and in your mouth, allowing you to cut away the dead flesh and hidden sin as you set yourself apart for God.

What Is Your "It"?

Over twenty years ago when the Lord first called me to preach, He showed me some things that were for a time and season yet to come. I could not walk into all of His promises at once, but I knew He would lead me in His will as I was willing to sanctify myself and follow Him. Recently, the Lord has stirred my spirit with a sense that now is the time. It is as if He is saying, "You've prayed about it. You've dreamed about it. You've asked Me for it. You've longed for it. It's been prophesied over you. Prepare yourself."

I traveled back to North Carolina, where I was born and raised. My grandfather still has a home in Middlesex, North Carolina. It is a beautiful mansionlike homestead set on acres of rolling, lush farmland with horses, cattle, and even his own private airstrip for his plane. Twenty-eight children were raised in that house over the years, and all of them serve the Lord.

During that special visit back to my roots, my heritage, I spent time each day walking that airstrip and the fields in prayer and communion with God. I felt the Holy Spirit's leading to visit the place down the road where He first called me to preach. I had not been back there in twenty-two years. I went down to that wonderful old Church of God sanctuary and sat down in the very spot of my calling. I can remember like it was yesterday. I was on a three-day fast, and I was crying out, "O God, can You use me? Why are You calling me to preach? I can't do it. I don't know how to preach. I'm afraid. I'm not worthy. I'm not good enough." I was giving Him all the excuses and all the fear. I didn't realize that during that three-day fast I was cutting off the flesh with a sharp knife.

Finally, on the third day, I heard His voice in my spirit say, "I've called you to preach. Go and do what I've called you to do." I said, "Lord, if this is truly Your will, then let my mother confirm it when I get home, even though it's past midnight. Let her be up and let her confirm it." I was young, and it never hurts to ask for clarity! I walked out of that tiny sanctuary weeping, got into my car, and drove barely a quarter mile home. When I walked back to Mom's bedroom, she was on her knees praying. As soon as I saw her, she whirled around, pointed her finger, and started speaking with stammering lips: "Jentezen, God has called you to preach. Go and do what He has called you to do."

> **God wants you to ask Him for things that are bigger than yourself!**

Sitting in that very same spot more than twenty years later, I was absolutely overwhelmed. Emotions like I have never felt before in my life washed over me. It was in that moment that I again sensed the leading of the Spirit in my heart directing me to fast and sanctify myself a second time because He had prophetically led me back to that spot where I started. He was about to begin a brand-new thing in my life. Like the children of Israel, it was as if He said, "You've never been this way before."

What About You?

What if you set yourself to diligently seek the Lord, sanctifying yourself with a fast and journey back to the spot where it all began—where He saved you, set you free, filled you with His Spirit, and called you out? I actually physically traveled to that spot, but if you cannot do that, you can go back mentally. You can recall the ancient landmark, that same simplicity, innocence, and dedication with which you first responded to His voice.

God wants you to ask Him for—believe Him for—things that are bigger than yourself. I am now over forty years old, but I cannot just float through life. I can't kick back and wait for retirement. I have too much promised! I want to reap the harvest. The children of Israel had made it through the wilderness. They had stopped eating manna and had begun to eat the good fruit of the land. They lived along a river, and they could have easily set up trade with those from the big city of Jericho, but that was not their destiny.

Fasting will bring you into destiny. Fasting will bring you into alignment with God's plan for your life. Just as Joshua called the children of promise to sanctify themselves—I believe that, likewise, your "tomorrow" is just around the corner. God is going to do wonders in your life, leading you places you have never been before. Now is the time to fast, to seek God diligently, to sanctify yourself, to discern God's priorities, and to walk in His promises. *Go for it!*

Notes

Chapter 2—Dethroning King Stomach

1. *Matthew Henry's Commentary*, "Numbers 11," http://www.htmlbible.com/kjv30/henry/H04C011.htm (accessed August 24, 2007).

Chapter 3—How Much? How Long? How Healthy?

1. Bob Rodgers, *101 Reasons to Fast* (Louisville, KY: Bob Rodgers Ministries, 1995), 52.

2. Don Colbert, MD, *Toxic Relief* (Lake Mary, FL: Siloam, 2003), 155.

3. Rodgers, *101 Reasons to Fast*, 53.

4. Ibid., 50–51.

5. Ibid., 50.

6. Ibid., 51.

Chapter 5—Swatting Flies

1. Richard Gazowsky, *Prophetic Whisper* (San Francisco, CA: Christian WYSIWYG Filmworks, 1998) 31–35.

2. Ibid.

3. Ibid.

4. Colbert, *Toxic Relief*, 30.

Chapter 7—You Shall Be Filled

1. Colbert, *Toxic Relief*, 32.

2. Ibid., 39.

About the Author

Jentezen Franklin is the pastor of Free Chapel in Gainesville, Georgia, a congregation that has 10,000 in attendance each week. Named as one of the top forty churches in America by *Outreach* magazine, Free Chapel has recently grown into a new location in Orange County, California, where Pastor Franklin also speaks weekly.

Through his experience as a pastor, teacher, musician, and author, Pastor Franklin seeks to help people encounter God through inspired worship and relevant application of the Word of God in their daily lives. His nationally televised program, *Kingdom Connection*, is seen weekly on prime-time television through various national and international networks.

Pastor Franklin is a popular speaker at numerous conferences across the country and around the world. He has also written several books, including the best sellers *Fasting Volume I: The Private Discipline That Brings Public Reward*, *Fasting Volume II: Opening a*

Door to God's Promises, and most recently, *Right People, Right Place, Right Plan,* which quickly became a best seller.

Pastor Franklin and his wife, Cherise, reside in Gainesville, Georgia, with their five wonderful children.

For more information, contact:

Jentezen Franklin Ministries
P. O. Box 315
Gainesville, GA 30503

Or visit us on the Web:

www.jentezenfranklin.org
www.freechapel.org